I0191905

Divatiel

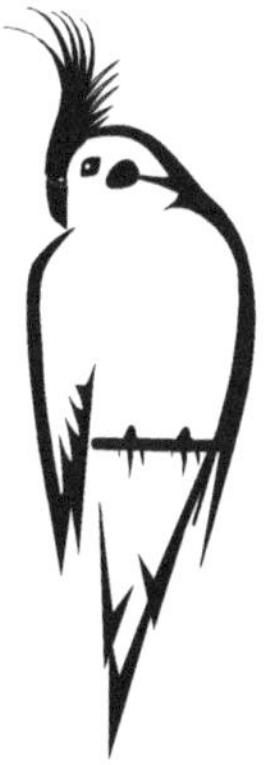

Divatiel

Reflections of a bird's companion

Cindi R. Maciolek

Grand Arbor Press, LLC

Las Vegas, Nevada
www.grandarborpress.com

Copyright © 2012 Cindi R. Maciolek
All rights reserved. No part of this publication may be reproduced, distributed or transmitted in any form or by any means, or stored in a database or retrieval system, without the prior written permission of the publisher.

Grand Arbor Press, LLC
1930 Village Center Circle
#3-388
Las Vegas, NV 89134

Visit our website for current contact information:
www.grandarborpress.com.

Grand Arbor Press, LLC books may be purchased for educational, business or sales promotional use. Please contact the company for more information.

Divatiel, the Divatiel logo and Divatiel bird icon are trademarks of Grand Arbor Press, LLC.

Printed in the United States of America.

First Printing: January 2012

Credits:
Cover design: Shelly Volsche
Front cover photo: Cindi R. Maciolek
Back cover photo: Jackie Carpenter

Library of Congress Control Number: 2011940754

Print Edition:
ISBN13: 978-0-9647911-3-8
ISBN10: 0-9647911-3-7

Electronic Edition:
ISBN13: 978-0-9647911-4-5
ISBN10: 0-9647911-4-5

To William

di•va•tiel [dee-*vuh* teel]

noun

Seriously, a *diva*-tastic cockatiel. Well loved. Very demanding. Alpha Bird. Queen of the Castle. With a great Mom.

Divatiel

Reflections of a bird's companion

Part One, San Jose, California

The Teeny Tiny Condo

Slightly Bigger House

Part Two, Las Vegas, Nevada

The Great Big House

Much Smaller House

Preface

My Little Divatiel

"She's the fattest cockatiel I've ever seen!"

Okay, that was the fourth vet to make the same comment. The average cockatiel weighs between 90 and 110 grams, and Jaké was generally 115-125. I didn't see what the big deal was. What's a few grams between friends…

"I don't clip her wings," I countered. "Those extra feathers must weigh something!"

I mean, we're talking half an ounce here. The feathers must have accounted for a few of those extra grams.

The vet seemed unconvinced.

"I allow her to fly around the house. She has great cardio," I added in her defense.

"So, now you're telling me it's muscle weight?" The vet nearly doubled over in laughter. "She's fat! Get over it!"

I packed up my princess in her cage and took her back to the palace, where she could eat her healthy food (vet prescribed, by the way), have her run of the house, and nap at her desire.

Fattest cockatiel, indeed, I thought. *She's not fat. She's just big boned.*

I knew my life was in for a big change when, just three seconds after I put Jaké on my shoulder, she had unhooked my necklace.

I had heard birds were intelligent, but I really had no idea just how smart they are. Generally, when people think of talented birds, they think of the large ones – parrots, macaws, even mynahs. No one pays attention to the little ones that can infiltrate every aspect of our lives when given the opportunity.

Jaké was an absolute blessing. Sure, she had her moments, but I'm certain she felt the same way about me. I never had children, so Jaké became my child. She was spoiled as much as you could possibly spoil a fine feathered friend, and her hours of blissful companionship were my reward.

While many pet owners carry around their designer dogs in custom made totes, I'm certain they have no idea what joy a cockatiel could bring into their lives, if they only allowed it. Or, maybe I just had the "*perfect storm*" of bird and owner and I'm very grateful for that.

Like a dog, Jaké was my faithful and loyal companion from the very first day we met. Like a dog, Jaké sat on my leg while I typed on my computer, nipping at my elbow when I moved and disturbed her naps. Like a dog, she sometimes chased her tail, particularly when a feather was ready to come out and it got stuck in an upright position, like a rudder on a plane. And, just like a dog, Jaké liked to take naps with her owner, picking the time and the place regardless of my plans for the day.

Jaké had her quirks, and just like humans, they changed over time. One that always made me laugh was how she hated to hear the sound of a utensil scraping a dish. I don't care where she was in the house – sometimes even sleeping in the bathroom – but as soon as she heard it, she started to yell!

She also found comfort in taking naps on the rungs of my office chair. Sometimes when I'd been out for the day, I'd go into my office to find her sound asleep, waiting for me to come home. You gotta love that.

It's been said that cockatiels have the brain power of a two-year-old child, and their behavior is not much different. If I wanted Jaké to stop doing something, I'd tell her, "No!" She'd acknowledge my request with a little chirp, but proceed on, totally ignoring me. She knew I didn't want her to do it, but she didn't care. Sound like a two-year-old, parents?

Like a kid, she hated the toys I bought her, preferring to rip up the boxes they came in. And, instead of sticky fingerprints on those nice greeting cards that were ready to mail, Jaké left a bite mark in every one of mine.

Since birds in the wild fly all the time, I never gave it a thought that they have to improve their cardio when the need arises, just like humans. When I moved from my tiny condo to a house with a really long hallway, Jaké would follow me to my office only to be winded for about five minutes, until she built up her stamina.

Jaké was never really like a bird; she was always more like a spoiled Diva, from the first moment I let her out of her cage and welcomed her into my household. My *Divatiel* discovered a side of herself that would have remained buried if not for the freedom she was given, and the communication we developed.

Most people don't realize just how much personality a little bundle of feathers can have, but I assure you, if you nurture the relationship, that personality will not only appear but will strengthen over time.

So few books have been written about pet birds, particularly from an owner's perspective, that I felt it was time to change that. Here's my account of life with the sweetest little thing to cross my path. Everything is to the best of my recollection although I've changed or omitted a few names. Jaké and I were together a long time, so I'm sure her version of some of the events would differ from mine, but I guess we'll never know.

Enjoy!

Part One
San Jose, California

The Teeny Tiny Condo

Chapter One

Searching for the right roommate

I always wanted a pet, but my Mom was never a dog or cat kind of person. She had six children, so she was reluctant to have the added responsibility of a furry little friend. When I was about eight years old, I was given two turtles. While not the cuddliest of creatures, I appreciated the opportunity to have something to call my own. Unfortunately, they lasted only six months before they departed for that huge aquarium in the sky. I also tried keeping goldfish but they didn't last either. I started to question my ability to raise anything besides ivy.

Just before I left for college, I made my way to the local K-Mart and came home with two parakeets in a brass cage. The yellow one I named Goldilocks; I can't remember the name of the other. They seemed to get along so well at the store, but within three days, Goldilocks had attacked the other bird and it was off to join my turtles and goldfish in pet heaven. At the time, I didn't realize just how territorial birds could be, so I went back to K-Mart and purchased a blue parakeet I named Bluebird, Boo-boo for short. The bird barely had time to learn its name when it, too, fell victim to Goldilocks and her protective ways. I'd known others who had parakeets and I didn't recall any such horror stories, but I quickly learned my lesson and Goldi was forever a solitary bird.

When I went off to college, Goldi wasn't allowed to live with me in the dorm, so I left her at home where she quickly bonded with my Dad. I'd come home on the weekends and it was as if she didn't even know I existed. But when my Dad entered the room, she had special tweets and chirps reserved just for him. Her eyes followed him everywhere, and whenever he came near her, she whistled and climbed all around the cage, hoping he would talk to her or give her special treats. She only had eyes for him. What once was mine now belonged to Dad.

I longed for that same connection with my own pet, but shortly after I graduated from college, I packed up my car and moved from Michigan to the Bay Area in California. Silicon Valley was booming at the time, and I was lucky enough to find a job soon after my arrival. I took a few years to get settled, switched jobs and bought my first place – a teeny, tiny condo in San Jose.

My position as marketing communications manager for a small software company meant I traveled a lot as well as put in long hours at the office when I was in town. As much as I enjoyed being on my own, I really wanted a pet to love and nurture. I definitely wasn't a cat person, but a small dog was a possibility. However, with my wee condo and traveling lifestyle, I didn't think it was fair to keep the poor thing locked up all day or in a kennel during my travels.

I knew that having a pet required committing to taking care of this little creature for its whole life, so I definitely wanted to choose the right one. I started researching all sorts of different animals and visited the pet stores every chance I got. No matter how often I eyed the dogs, I was most fascinated by the birds, many of which live a very long life.

One store had a huge cage of hand-fed cockatiels (*Nymphicus hollandicus*) that appeared to be calm, sweet and loving. They were a bit more interactive than the parakeet I'd had when I was younger, yet they were easier to take care of than a dog. I didn't need to be home every couple of hours to let them outside for a potty break so cockatiels could survive my long work days, and I felt they would be easier to board when I was out of town. I thought a cockatiel would be more portable and fit my lifestyle perfectly.

The more time I kept them company at the pet store, the more I was convinced I was making the right decision. But, before I could spend the money and bring one home, I was on a plane, heading to some high tech destination around the world.

One day at the office, I shared my desire for a pet bird with a co-worker, William, who happened to have a cockatiel at home that was annoying him.

"It's so messy," said the neat freak. "And it yells every morning as soon as the sun comes up. It's so noisy!"

"Birds are messy," I said. "Didn't you know that when you bought it?"

"I didn't buy this one," he said. "It was a gift."

"Oh." That explained a lot. The worst thing in the world is to buy a pet for someone who doesn't want it. "Is it a boy or a girl?" I asked.

"I think it's a boy," he said. "I never took it to the vet, so I don't know."

Hmmm...

"What's his name?" I asked.

"I never gave him a name," he said.

"Never gave him a name! How cruel is that!" I was shocked. "How long have you had him?"

"He's four years old, and I've had him since he was a baby," he said. "He's really messy and noisy."

"But cockatiels are so cute," I beamed. After some careful thought, I added, "If you ever want to get rid of him, I'll take him."

"I don't think so, not right now," he said, "but I'll keep that in mind."

A few weeks went by with lots of travel, but no bird. Then, one Friday I walked into my office and there, underneath my desk, was a brass cage with a scared little cockatiel. He was so adorable! His body was grey with rosy red cheeks, like someone put blush on him. He had bits of yellow around the eyes and at the base of his long, curly plume. White trimmed the edges of his wings, and his tail feathers were a fabulous pattern of grey, white and yellow. I'd never seen a more beautiful sight! I pulled the cage onto my desk, and leapt for joy!

I ran down the hall to William's office, yelling, "Thank you! Thank you! Thank you!"

"You can have him," he said as we walked back to my office. My new little baby was shaking in his feathers, but seemed sweet as could be.

"Here, he likes to have his head scratched, like this." William stuck his finger through the cage and sure enough, the bird bent his head and tilted side to side while William scratched it, a move that would repeat with me for years to come.

"I've already named him," I said. "I'm going to call him Jake."

"Jake! Why Jake?" he asked.

"I don't know. That name just stuck in my head whenever I thought about the bird," I replied.

It just felt right to me at the time, so I went with it. In short order, the name would be transformed to accommodate the reality of its sex.

With that, my co-worker shrugged his shoulders and went back to his office to work. Jake and I were left to bond in my office, welcoming visitors until it was time to head home.

Thus began the second longest relationship in my life, just behind the potted palm I got in 1985.

Chapter Two

The roommate moves in

"OK, Jake, let's go home."

It was Friday afternoon about 2 p.m., a little early for me to call it a weekend. However, it seemed every time I left my office, even for just a second, Jake would start chirping very loudly. Rather than disrupt my co-workers, or the owners of the company, any longer, I decided to pack up my new baby and introduce him to his new house. Besides, his cage took up most of my desk so it was hard to work, and whenever I looked at the little cutie, he would bend his head down for me to scratch. Better we just go home and get to know each other.

I carried Jake's cage down the stairs and put it on the front seat of my little sports car. It was a tight fit, but manageable. I got in on the driver side and drove the mile back to the condo. Once inside my one-car garage, it was another feat to get the cage out of the car. There was barely enough room for me to exit my auto, let alone Jake! Eventually, I'd learn to park as far to the right as I could to allow ample room whenever I needed to transport my little bundle of feathers.

Once inside, the cage seemed enormous in my teeny, tiny condo. In reality, it wasn't that big, but it did take up one of the most valuable resources in my kitchen: clean counter space. I left Jake there to assess his surroundings while I went to get the mail. I could hear him outside, chirping, and I hoped my neighbors would forgive me while Jake adjusted.

"OK, little guy," I said while opening the cage door. "Let's see how you'll do with a little freedom."

I put my hand inside and quickly Jake scurried away from it. He tried to climb all around and upside down, hissing and yelling the whole time. He was afraid, but I hoped he would get over it soon enough.

Eventually, Jake plopped onto my hand. He tried to fly the instant he was out of the cage, but his wings were clipped so he dropped to the floor. He tried again to build up some momentum, but without his long wing feathers, he couldn't go very far. My heart was broken! A bird should be able to fly.

I know most people clip a bird's wings out of fear that they'll fly away. They can also fly into walls, mirrors, windows and other things and hurt themselves. Or, they can get into trouble by hanging out on tops of doors and eating the wood or by getting their feet caught when the door is closed quickly. I'd also heard of birds being stepped on because although they can fly, they also like to walk on the floor. If the bird is in the cage, you don't have to worry about such things.

However, I hated to see Jake suffer. The look in his eyes tore at my heart strings. What if there was an emergency and he couldn't save himself? Or, if he fell and he couldn't fly to reach his food? I didn't want him to bond with me because he *had* to. I wanted him to feel like part of the family, to bond with me because he *wanted* to. For the most part, Jake would be in the cage when I wasn't home and only out of the cage when I was.

I decided right then and there I wasn't going to clip his wings after his next molt, to let him be a real bird, not just a pet. In bird terms, that's called *being flighted*. I would be his flock, but he would also have the opportunity to fly up on cabinets or onto my shoulder as he chose, not forced to bond with me because his wings were clipped.

Not everyone can deal with this, and if I changed my mind, control was just a quick snip away. But, in my heart, I wanted him to be as normal as possible within the confines of our house. Jake would be flighted the rest of his life. I really had no idea what I was getting myself into when I made that first decision, but I still believe it was the right one.

I scooped Jake up off the floor, and put him on my shoulder while I read my mail. About three seconds later, I felt something drop down the front of my blouse. In three short seconds, Jake had undone the clasp of my necklace! Somehow, he figured out how to unhook the extra-security clasp he had never seen before, and felt very proud of it. I could see now my life was in for a big change.

While I tried to pick up the necklace, he was already working on my earrings. "Jake, you little snot!" I said as I took him off my shoulder and placed him on top of his cage. "I can't believe you just did that!" I quickly removed all my jewelry and put it safely away.

Jake sat quietly atop his cage, taking in his surroundings. He walked from side to side, looking up, down and around, not sure where he was, surveying the land. He still quivered but I would, too, if suddenly I was packed up and moved from a home I'd known for four years. And, since he'd never been out of the cage before, this certainly was a whole new experience.

I changed my clothes in my bedroom and came back into the kitchen to search for a vet in the phone book. Immediately, I located a bird specialist whose office was just a few miles away. How serendipitous! I picked up Jake, put him on my shoulder, grabbed the phone and sat down on the sofa to make his first appointment.

"Hi! I have a new member of the family I'd like to bring in."

"Sure. What type of bird is it?"

"It's a cockatiel, four years old. A grey one."

"OK, the doctor can see you on Tuesday at 4 p.m. What is your bird's name?"

Aha! If William had taken the bird to a vet, he would have had a name. Vets always ask what the pet's name is.

"Jake," I averred.

"OK, we'll see you and Jake on Tuesday."

I hung up the phone and noticed Jake was now at the nape of my neck, biting the label on my shirt. I had to maneuver to reach him back there, and he knew it. I eventually was able to coax him onto my hand, and sat him on my knee, whereupon he bowed his head and waited for me to scratch it. When William did it, I thought it was some sort of magic trick. Now I realize it's not only part of the bonding experience, it's also a necessary part of the preening process.

I scratched Jake's head for at least two hours, his head turning and twisting to make sure I got all the right spots. A little to the left. A little to the right. Just above the eye. Behind the ear. Under the chin. Above the beak. If I tried to take my hand away, he would nip at it. How dare I even consider! I was there to serve, and this should have been my first indication. But, no! I hadn't a clue.

By then, I think we were both exhausted from all the excitement of the day. I lay down on my comfortable leather sofa, Jake on my chest. We began a ritual that would serve us all the days of our lives – we took our first nap together.

I soon discovered just how often a cockatiel drops, or goes to the bathroom. Call it what you want, but it's about once every 20 minutes. Cockatiel droppings are small, circular green and white gifts that are not only a normal part of their waste system, they can also be a first indication if something is wrong.

Now, the droppings might be small, and they certainly are compared to larger birds, but they are frequent. If a dropping is fresh, a wet tissue will wipe it away quickly. If you let it dry, it will fall off in a clump but will leave behind a creamy residue that can be cleaned with a wet tissue. Lesson: have lots of wet tissues on hand!

After that first experience, I would not recommend wearing your better clothes if you want your bird to hang with you. I could tell already it was time to set aside a wardrobe of old t-shirts to wear around the house so I wouldn't have to worry. That day, however, I let it slide. It was a special day, after all – Jake's first day in his new home!

We spent the rest of the evening quietly getting to know each other. We watched television. We ate. I scratched Jake's head. Then I discovered one of the most magical and mesmerizing activities a bird does: preening. It was almost meditative to watch him smooth and clean his feathers with his beak. Some folks have aquariums because they like to watch the fish swim. It's a very calming experience. Me, I liked to watch Jake preen. For hours. It was such a beautiful sight.

Eventually, it was time for both of us to go to sleep. William said he never covered his cage, so I wasn't about to start. When it was nite-nite time, I simply put Jake in his cage, and put it on top of my dresser in the bedroom. No sweat! He fell asleep right away, slept all night, and even slept in on Saturday. William said he was noisy and woke up early. I guess William just didn't have the sleeping vibe!

The next morning, Jake seemed a little more his true self after the excitement of the previous day. However, I was starting to have doubts about whether this was, indeed, a male bird. If you think about it, males tend to strut around, puffing out their chests, trying to look all studly, with an air about them that says, "I'm bad. Don't mess with me."

This bird, on the other hand, had more female reactions. Even though he was friendly and loving, he was more skittish, wanting attention but only when he allowed it, yelling at me in a way only a female could.

"Don't touch me! Go away! I'll let you know when I want to bond," translated, "Chirp chirp chirp chirp chirp! Hiss! Hiss! Chirp chirp," then bowing his head so I could scratch it.

In due time, *he* would prove to be a *she*, but for now, all I wanted to do was make friends with my new roommate.

Chapter Three

Our first vet visit

That following Tuesday, I toted my precious little Jake, like a proud Mommy, into the vet's office. This particular vet specialized in birds. In fact, that's all she treated. How lucky I was to live so near her.

She took one look at Jake, and decided to do a full-on exam. Sounded good to me! Blood test, gram stain, and whatever else she felt necessary. I wanted Jake to have a clean bill of health. And, by doing a full exam right at the beginning, we had a benchmark for future exams so we could track any changes. A lot of these terms and tests were foreign to me, but I was a quick study and soon learned all the important details of raising a healthy bird.

The gram stain takes some droppings and does an analysis to see if there's any bacterial infection. That was easy. The vet simply took a long swab and picked up some of Jake's droppings from the bottom of his cage and smeared it onto a microscope slide.

The blood test gives a reading on all sorts of good things like kidney function, calcium level and so on. That was a little harder to watch. The vet clipped a toe nail until it bled, and put the teeniest vial I'd ever seen underneath it to catch the blood.[1] In fact, she took three vials. Was there any blood left in the bird? The vet was able to do the gram stain analysis right away, but the blood work results would take a few days.

"You're lucky you brought him in," the vet said. "He has such a bad bacterial infection he would have died if you waited much longer. And he's very dehydrated."

"Oh, my gosh, you're kidding me! Can it be treated?" I was worried. I'd just taken him under my wing, and already it was bad news.

"Yes, I'll give him some fluids and some other medicine. I'll need to see him again in a couple of days to see how he's doing and

[1]Words from my vet: Nowadays, blood is typically taken from the jugular vein of the bird, as this tends to be less painful and stressful.

to give you the results of his blood test. He's also suffering from a vitamin deficiency. You can tell because his throat and nostrils are bright red."

She seemed very concerned, and now I was motherly worried. I watched as she grabbed a teeny syringe of fluids and placed it into his wings. It puffed up like a little bubble but it eventually worked its way into his system. That would help with his dehydration.

"What are you feeding him?" she asked.

I told her what William gave me, and she nearly threw up.

"Dump it all! You need to give him quality food. In fact, he should be living only on pellets. He'll fight you, but you have to be the boss and eventually, he'll convert. You could also give him some seed cakes that are loaded with pellets. Sometimes it's easier to convert them when you do it that way."

Yikes! Lots of changes all at once, not only for me, but for Jake as well. He seemed to look healthy, but now that she had made the diagnosis, it was as if he felt relieved, that he didn't have to hide it anymore. Birds hide their sicknesses really well because they don't want to be seen as the weakest link in the flock. They can put on a good front but, in actuality, they might be gravely ill. Such was the case with my little one.

"Are you going to keep his wings clipped?" she asked.

"No, I want him to be able to fly," I said. "He's a bird, after all!"

I smiled, but the vet just stared at me. Her look was somewhere between disbelief and anger.

"That's fine, but know that you're taking on a major responsibility by not clipping his wings," she stated emphatically. "Birds can get into a lot of trouble. Are you prepared for that?"

Now *I* was shaking in my skin. "Yes, ma'am," I replied, although at that moment she had me really worried.

"You'll also have to bring him in every two or three months to trim his nails," she said. "They can get caught when they're too long. If they get pulled out, the bird can bleed to death. Birds are basically skin, tiny bones, feathers and about a thimble full of blood. It doesn't take much to harm them."

OK, I thought. *I'll put it in my calendar every two months to have a nail trim.*

The vet eyed me up and down before she spoke.

"Birds are wonderful creatures, but they are very sensitive and need to have the right care to live a long and healthy life."

I took her comments to heart and vowed I'd do everything I could to be a good mother for Jake.

In addition to the diagnosis and the food directives, the vet gave me a list of instructions I was commanded to follow.

"If you don't adhere to my rules, don't bother coming back," she stated.

I had heard too many birds are considered throw away pets, so owners don't give them the care they truly need. And, since something like less than 10 percent of pet owners have birds, you really needs to find a vet with avian experience to get the right guidance. She was very strict but as time went on, I realized how important her rules were for both me and my baby. I'm certain it helped to contribute to Jake's long life.

She handed me a sheet of paper and went over the key points.

No chocolate or avocado. *Check.*

Let him sleep at least 10 hours a night in a dark place. *Check.*

Feed him fresh vegetables daily. *Check.*

I thought I could handle the rules, although these were only the tip of the iceberg.

"I'm serious," she said. "I'll ask you a few questions on your next visit. If I ascertain you're not following the rules, I won't ever treat your bird again."

OK, then.

Since I was there, I thought I'd bring up the subject of sex.

"Can you tell if it's a boy or a girl?"

I related my hypothesis, and she just laughed.

"It's often hard to tell with birds. Sometimes, unless they lay eggs, you can't totally be certain. I say, go with your gut on this one."

And so I did. Jake became Jaké before I left the office.

So, why Jaké you ask?

It really wasn't up to me. Computers at that time weren't as sophisticated as they are today, and once a pet's name was entered into the record, you couldn't change it but you could append it. I didn't want a female bird named Jake, and I didn't like the technician's suggestion of adding an E to the name to make it Jakee, so I decided to add an accent after the E. She instantly became Jake', *Divatiel.*

I never thought there'd be any problem with her name, but just like her Mom's, it gets misspelled all the time. Since it's pronounced (ja-kay′) people spell it like it sounds. Or, as they *think* I should spell it. No matter how many times I say J-A-K-E with an accent after the E, I get Jackay, Jacke, Jacké, Jackée, Jacquée, Jakée, Jakay and any other assorted spellings. Even for ease of writing this book, I've spelled it incorrectly by placing the accent above the E rather than after it.

Luckily, she couldn't read...

Chapter Four

On the mend

When we got home from that first office visit, we were both exhausted once again. Jaké really looked sick. She was all puffed up, huddled on her perch and her eyes were closing. I was so worried she was not going to live. She pretty much slept the next three days straight, whether with me or on her own in her cage. And she ate and drank. Other than that, there was very little activity in *Divatieldom.*

I took Jaké back to the vet a few days later for the results of her blood test. The vet performed another gram stain analysis, and once again injected fluids into Jaké's wings to help with her dehydration. She also gave her some calcium.

"You have to be careful how much calcium you give to a bird," she said. "If you give them too much at once, it can cause a heart attack. She's so little, you just need a tiny bit."

Great, I thought. *Just what I need. More things to worry about.*

I was a wreck, and so was my little birdie.

We returned home and I tried to be as relaxed and loving as I could. I had so many details to remember from the vet, and I watched Jaké like a hawk. If there was any little change, I wanted to be aware and make my way back to the vet to address it right away.

I didn't realize it at the time, but Jaké could pick up how I was feeling, and I'm sure that made her even more anxious than she already was. But as the days passed, I started to notice less puffiness and sleeping, more yelling and activity. My baby was on the mend and I was calming down.

I had to work during the week, so I left the lights and the radio on at home while I was in the office. I decided to play various styles of music to see if she reacted differently to them. I'm not sure if it's a quirk of the breed or just personal taste, but Jaké definitely had a preference for certain types of music.

I realized that if she listened to country or big band, she was in a good mood when I came home. But, if I left her with classic rock, easy listening or even classical, she was a bit grumpy when I opened the door. I wanted her rested but active when I got home, so country and big band turned out to be the genres of choice. Luckily, I lived in a part of the country that had so many wonderful options on the radio.

I also noticed that when I played Lorie Line piano music, it put her right to sleep. (Note to mothers: It might just work on babies!) If I particularly needed Jaké to calm down so I could get some work done, on went the Lorie Line and in a wink she was fast asleep.

She didn't hate all classical music. Ballet music seemed to be okay with her. It wasn't as relaxing as Lorie Line, but it didn't make her grumpy. She also tolerated my love of The Beatles and Madonna.

I took the vet's advice and bought lettuce, parsley and cucumber to add variety and vitamins to her diet. I cut small pieces and put them on top of her cage so they were easy for her to reach. At first, she cowered from them being on top of her, as if an invasion of her private space. But when she nipped at them and realized they actually tasted good, she thought of them as treats and looked forward to fresh ones every day.

We developed a pretty boring routine. I'd leave for work around 9 a.m., and return around 7 p.m. We'd watch television, eat, I'd scratch her head, then it was nite-nite time. On occasion, she wanted to go nite-nite as soon as I got home, which made the vet happy but me a little sad because after a long day at work, I looked forward to our time together. However, I knew Jaké needed to get well, so the more she slept, the more she healed.

The more *she* healed, the more my wallet healed as well. Owning a bird is not for the faint of pocketbook. The bird was given to me for free, but a month later with vet bills and new food, I was $550 invested into my new companion.

Before I knew it, I had to head out on a business trip. Surprisingly, I'd been home for nearly a month. I worked for a high tech company in Silicon Valley, and I travelled about 50 percent of the time, so a month home was a luxury. I packed my bags, hopped on a plane, and another co-worker came by every day to feed Jaké and check to make sure she was OK.

In addition to knowing how to care for a bird and having a great vet, it's also critical to find the right people to take care of her should you need to travel. Some people will do it for free, others you need to pay. I've made some good choices and some not so good. You live and learn.

This co-worker lived nearby, and since my condo was close to the office, she would stop by on her way in to work to open the blinds, turn on the radio and give Jaké fresh food, water and treats. On her way home, she closed the blinds, turned off the radio and left a night light on. The whole time I was out of town, Jaké stayed in the cage.

After a week, I was back, and slowly, I could see Jaké was getting stronger and feeling better. I felt guilty for being away, so I did what any mother would do: I bought her gifts. I read how smart cockatiels were, so I wanted Jaké to find something to pique her interest outside of the cage besides me. After a lot of research, I settled on a wooden gym. It was a perch with a ladder, a food dish, and a swing.

She detested it! Every time I put her on the perch, she freaked. She'd sit very erect, her plume high on her head, a look of fear in her eyes. I put food on there, tried to get her to see it as a fun thing, but she would have no part of it. I couldn't believe it. I took her rejection personally, and researched other toys that might make her happy. I should have stopped buying her gifts after her bitter reaction to this initial purchase, but a mother always wants to spoil her children.

Turns out, Jaké hated normal bird toys. They were beneath her. The gym was step one. I took a picture of her on it, and I think I could count on one hand the number of times she actually sat on the perch. Off it went to Goodwill.

Then, I thought she needed a pal to keep her company while

I was at work. I bought her a small, plastic bobbing bird, kind of like kids' Weebles. She just looked at it, assumed it was renting out the bottom of her cage, and there it sat, untouched by the *Divatiel*. However, when I cleaned her cage, I had to put the bobbing bird back in; otherwise she yelled at me, but she wouldn't go near it.

Same thing with a mirror and bell. I haven't heard of a bird that doesn't like to look at her reflection in the mirror. Well, my little *Divatiel* didn't. Whether it was the small hanging mirror in her cage or the large one in my bathroom, she always thought the bird in the mirror was out to get her. Whenever she saw her reflection, she hissed at it and scurried to my opposite shoulder, rather than flirting with it.

From Jaké's perspective, the only things she needed in life were food, water, sleep, a warm home…and ME!

You know the old joke about yesterday's news becoming today's birdcage liner? Well, it's not always that simple.

Since Jaké spent so much time in her cage, it was important for me to keep it clean. In addition to giving her fresh food, water and treats every day, I emptied the dirty newspaper that lined the bottom of the cage and replaced it with a fresh, clean sheet.

You can tell when something bothers a cockatiel because their plume goes up and their eyes are always focused on the item that is irritating them at that moment. I never thought clean newspaper would be a source of irritation, but one morning I changed her paper and immediately her plume went up and her head tilted to the side.

I wasn't paying a lot of attention to her, but I noticed she hadn't really moved since I cleaned her cage.

"What's up, Jaké? What are you looking at?"

I tried to follow her gaze up. Since she had eyes on either side of her head, when her head was tilted, you were never sure if she was looking up or down. The bottom of the kitchen cabinet was above her and it was perfectly fine. So, I followed her gaze down into her cage. I couldn't imagine anything could be wrong. I had just cleaned it, for goodness sake!

But, when I took a good look, I realized the source of her irritation. There, in the middle of the newspaper, in bright color, was a picture. Without thinking, all the previous days I had used the classifieds to line her cage. Today, I just grabbed the front page. Big mistake!

"You silly girl! It's just a picture."

Jaké was unconvinced. Once she realized that I had figured out what was wrong, she started yelling at me.

"Fix it! Get rid of it! Chirp! Chirp! Chiiirrrppp!!!"

"OK, OK, hang on a second."

I took out the bottom tray, put the front page into the recycle bin, found the classified section, relined the tray and put it back into the cage. I immediately got the *"Chirp" of understanding*, and down she climbed to have breakfast.

Ah, children…

Chapter Five

The battle to change her food

Every day with Jaké was a new experience. We were definitely getting into a routine, but there were still some marching orders from the vet that I needed to deal with. It was time to get down to business.

The rules from my vet were relatively easy to follow, but her biggest concern was making sure Jaké ate good quality food. I thought it would be a simple switch. Instead of putting seed from the bag into her dish, I'd simply use the seed cakes and pellets I bought from the vet. However, changing Jaké's food was a battle I wasn't prepared for. Just imagine...it's Thanksgiving morn, your mother has decided to become a vegan and that's Tofurky in the oven.

Jaké had been eating what humans might consider fast food for four years. Cheap, plentiful, low on nutrition but certainly tasty. Now, the vet wanted me to feed her the equivalent of five star spa cuisine. Being the *Divatiel* that she was, you'd think she would have gone for the best right off the bat. But, no!

I decided to start the food transition on a Saturday so I could be home and monitor her reaction. Maybe I should have done it on a weekday so I could avoid her yelling!

I took a deep breath and emptied her two food dishes. In each of them, I put small green pellets on the bottom, then large blue pellets on top. I didn't know which she would like, if any, so I thought I'd give her options. They not only looked dramatically different from what she was used to, I'm certain they smelled different as well. The vet told me the pellets were a better option for her, so I held off using the seed cakes at first.

Jaké was on top of her cage, eyeing me as I made the switch. She usually ate about 30 minutes after we got up, so I could gauge when she was hungry. I tried to coax her inside to eat, but she was reluctant to come onto my hand. Something was different, she could sense it, and my anxiety certainly wasn't helping things. Jaké finally gave in and hopped onto my hand.

I put her on her perch, watching and waiting for her to climb down to her food dish. I normally didn't watch her, so maybe all the attention caught her off guard. I tried to play it cool and stepped away from her cage, but that didn't work.

Eventually, Jaké slid from her perch down to her food dish, didn't recognize what was in there, climbed back up on her perch and yelled – incessantly! My head hurt. "CHIRP! CHIRP! CHIRPCHIRPCHIRP CHIIIRRRPPP!!!" Birds are very much creatures of habit, and changing something as critical to her survival as the type of food she was eating was a major issue.

"She'll put up a fight," the vet had said, "but she'll be fine. Don't give in. Eventually, she'll eat the good stuff."

Don't give in! That was easy for her to say. If I hadn't been traveling so much, I might not have felt so guilty. But, I wasn't spending that much time with her as it was. How dare I not keep her company, then swap out her food! The nerve!

It was almost as if I could read Jaké's mind.

"What kind of Mommy are you? Where's my food? I don't recognize that stuff that's in my dish. I want my food back! Are you trying to starve me? What kind of trick are you playing on me? Give me my food back! CHIIIIRP!"

She just wouldn't stop yelling.

I spoke calmly to her as she screamed at me.

"It's OK, Jaké. This is good stuff. The doctor says it's good for you. Do you know how lucky you are to be eating such great food? You'll get used to it, Mommy promises."

She didn't buy it. Those initial screeches were followed by even more demanding shrills.

"You evil stepmother! I come here and give you all my love and what do I get? Don't you love me? How could you do this to me? Life was good before. Why do you have to change EVERYTHING! CHIIIIRRRRPP!"

I couldn't handle the screams any more. Supposedly, it takes about three days to convert a bird from seed to pellets, but I didn't have the heart to force it on her. She'd been through so much, been so ill when I first got her. Now I was traveling all the time. I just couldn't bear to listen to her cries.

I caved. I did the compromise thing. I put just a little seed in her food cup, added some small green pellets, then I crumbled a few seed cakes mixed with more green pellets on top of that. In another dish, I left the big blue pellets, the kind that larger birds eat.

I stepped away from the counter, sat on the sofa and let her be. She screamed a little more, but then she noticed that now there was something different in her food dish along with the regular seeds. She decided to take a chance, slid down the side of the cage and stuck her beak into the dish.

At first, she dug for her familiar seeds, but I noticed her nibbling on the seed cakes. I never once saw her try the little green pellets during her entire life, but today, for every two or three familiar seeds she ate, she took a bite from a seed cake. Must have tasted pretty good because the longer she ate, the more the ratio changed in favor of the seed cakes. I was so relieved!

As time went on, she always devoured the seed cakes and, although they weren't the perfect food, they were significantly better than what she had before. They also were far more expensive – about seven dollars for a package that would last four or five days, compared to a big bag of seed for seven dollars that would last at least a month.

I still hoped and prayed she would learn to like the pellets because the vet said they had all the vital nutrients she needed. And, I had already opened the packages. Since I couldn't return them, I decided to use them. Yet, every day I watched her eat and she still focused on the seed cakes and ignored the pellets. I felt as if I was throwing my money in the trash because she didn't eat the pellets, but as long as I put them in the food dish, my hope was that she would ultimately be tempted to try them.

One day, I was sitting on the sofa and Jaké was eating in her cage, as usual, with the door open. She loved to throw the seed cakes out of her dish onto the counter where she'd eat for a little change of pace.

Then a funny thing happened. I looked up, and there, in her claw, was a big blue pellet! She was nibbling on it almost like a rabbit with a carrot. She ate what she wanted from that one, threw it down, and grabbed another! She then went to her seed cakes and grabbed them the same way. She ate like that almost up to her 20th birthday.

Chapter Six

Sleeping and preening

Once we got past the food episode, life once again settled into a routine, at least when I was in town. I truly appreciated the days I was home with Jaké all day because I really got to know her and discover new things about her.

One thing that amazed me was how much and how long she ate. I didn't pay a lot of attention in the beginning because there was so much to learn, but once she was hooked on the seed cakes, she seemed to really eat a lot!

She, like me, was not a morning person, so it took about 30 minutes for her to decide to eat breakfast. Then, lunch came around 3 p.m., dinner around 7 p.m., and if we were up really late, a snack around 9:30 p.m. (I never told her vet!)

Each meal lasted approximately 20-30 minutes as she dug through her food dish, took a quick break for a sip of water, then climbed atop her cage to grab some treats. After a mini-break, she'd head down to her food dish again and finish off her meal.

I calculated that she ate approximately one and a half to two ounces of food a day, about half her body weight. So if anyone says you should eat like a bird, don't do it!

Sleeping was another interesting habit. I'd never really thought about how much birds slept, but by watching my little baby I determined that she slept quite a bit. There was her post-breakfast nap, her post-lunch nap, her pre-dinner nap and her pre-bedtime nap! In the wild, they spend hours foraging for food, but when it's provided, you have to do something with your time. Thus, napping was Jaké's favorite hobby, just ahead of head scratching.

Jaké certainly liked to sleep. She was my kind of bird from the very beginning. No getting up early for either of us. However, on occasion, I had to work late. Sometimes I didn't make it back home until 10 o'clock at night, way too late for the little princess to get her beauty sleep. In fact, I was severely reprimanded several times by our vet for not getting her to bed when the sun went down. In the winter, that can be 4:30 p.m. Way too early for even the heartiest sleepers, especially when you live with a night owl like me.

When Jaké first moved in, she slept in her cage at night. I'd take her out for a bit when I got home from work. Then, when I saw that her eyes were closing and she was all cuddled up in her sleepytime stance, I'd put her inside the cage and close the door. I placed her cage on top of the bureau in my bedroom, up a little higher than a table, so she could keep an eye on me and things around us. Birds are always skittish, so they like to have a bird's eye view of things.

Eventually, when Jaké was ready for nite-nite, she just yelled at me. It wasn't a normal yell, but rather a nite-nite screech; louder and more demanding. Not quite the same intonation of a "You forgot to give me my treats!" yell, or a "Why didn't you tell me the gardener was coming today!" chirp. It had its own sense of urgency, and was usually coupled with a bobbing head and a look in the direction of my bedroom.

I recalled that William had told me that she was always up early making lots of noise. From day one, I had not one single experience of the sort. I soon realized that she liked to sleep in, as did I, so the blinds were closed oftentimes until noon. When it was finally time for Mom to get up, so did Jaké, at which time she'd yell at me to bring her into the kitchen.

I attempted to put Jaké nite-nite as early as possible, heeding the words from our wonderful vet, but alas, my schedule didn't always work that way. However, as I was at work for several hours, Jaké was able to get in her beauty rest by napping in monumental amounts. No wonder she was such a cutie pie!

Jaké was capable of sleeping nearly anywhere, but her favorite place was with me on our big, comfy sofa.

I'd come home from work, turn on the TV, and before you knew it, we were sound asleep. Jaké found various positions for *her* comfort. Mostly, she cuddled into my neck, just under my hair.

It was as if my hair became a nest that she didn't have to build. Another favorite spot was right on my chest. That way, the second she sensed movement, she would bow her head, in easy reach for me to scratch it.

I loved when she'd sleep on the pillow, resting her beak in the crook of my nose. When I'd open my eyes, her face would light up as if to say, "Yippee! Mom's up!"

But, sometimes Jaké just wasn't as tired as I was. She'd nap for a bit, but then she'd decide it was play time, or time to for me to scratch her head. I'd be sound asleep when suddenly she'd start preening my eyelashes! Her little beak would go eyelash by eyelash, just like she preened her feathers. It would take about three eyelashes to wake me up. Then, she'd stop and give me that "Mom's up!" look. She'd bow her head ready for me to scratch it.

The most important aspect of our relationship was that Jaké liked to sleep as much as I do. Whether it was naps or just sleeping in on the weekend, we were definitely on the same wavelength. Sometimes we'd sleep till noon on a Saturday. I have no idea why William was complaining; she slept just fine at my house.

Anyone who has ever met a true *Divatiel* understands that they are a bit eccentric. They are very demanding, create ways to test you to make sure you understand they are number one, and have a number of quirks that can change as often as the wind blows.

When I responded to Jaké's wishes, she became the Alpha Bird, definitely in charge of the household. And, if I didn't respond, she continued to screech louder and louder until I took action. Sort of like humans visiting a foreign country where they don't speak the language. They think if you yell something loudly enough in English, the other party will understand. My little *Divatiel* was no different.

Preening was an avian activity I loved, but it definitely left Jaké in control. Preening is not just a beauty routine with birds, like women brushing their hair 100 times before they go to bed. Every day she had to work the oils on her feathers, from body to feather tip. One by one, inch by inch, every single feather, every day. She would bend and fluff and sometimes even sneeze.

The level of concentration she had when she did this was amazing, regardless of where she was. If she happened to be on my knee or my shoulder when she began, I was stuck! I'd have to sit or stand until she got to the point where she could take a break or else I got yelled at and bitten. Talk about control issues…

The only feathers she couldn't reach were on the top of her head and neck. In the wild, her partner would preen those for her. A captive bird relies on the owner to scratch her head. It's the closest thing to preening those feathers that she can get.

Jaké could have had me scratch her head every waking minute, except for when she was eating. She *loved* to have her head scratched! So, instead of becoming a fun bonding exercise, it was actually a way for the *Divatiel* to control me.

When Jaké was ready, she simply bowed her head. If she was anywhere on me – shoulder, knee, hand – and I didn't respond immediately, she nipped me a little bit and gave a huffy chirp. If I ignored her, she yelled a bit louder, then bowed her head when she saw me looking at her, watching me with the *Evil Eye.* If I continued to go about my business, she started biting and yelling really loudly. At that point, I usually stopped what I was doing to satisfy the *Divatiel's* wishes.

When she was really desperate, she simply rubbed her head along my neck. It tickled so much, it was hard for me not to move while she was doing it, especially when I knew the alternative was painful bites from her little beak.

However, with Jaké, you never knew from moment to moment where you stood. *She loves me, she hates me, she loves me, she hates me.* I'd be scratching her head, and suddenly she'd decide she didn't like the way I was doing it, so she'd step away and bite me. Not two seconds later, she'd be right back under my finger with her head tipped down, ready for another round.

If she was in a good mood, that round could easily have lasted an hour or so. She'd twist and turn her head so I could reach all the feathers. *A little to the left. A little to the right. Just above the eye. At the nape of the neck.* And on and on it would go. Jaké didn't care that I had other things to do. From her perspective, I had only one concern, and that was her.

If I was busy at my computer and I couldn't scratch her head, she'd either sit on my shoulder or on my knee, and sleep. Every time I moved, she nibbled on my neck or my elbow, just to be annoying. Oh, and I'm sure, to remind me that I was missing out on bonding time!

However, perhaps to make me jealous, Jaké identified a substitute. There were times when her intelligence took over and she realized that no matter how much of a fit she threw, I just couldn't scratch her head at the moment. So, she turned to that which would.

I'm not talking about another person, I'm talking about a static substitute. I had a small vase that has some raised leaves on it. They seemed to be the right height and shape to perfectly scratch her head. I'd see her moving her head and neck side to side, upside down and around, until she noticed that I was available. Then she would stop, yell at me and go back to her vase, perhaps trying to make me jealous.

Sometimes, I got annoyed with all the demands of my little *Divatiel*. So, whenever I thought she was misbehaving, I'd say, "I'm going to send you back to William!" She'd look at me with a shocked expression on her face, stiffen her back and raise the plume on top of her head. She knew what it meant, and I guess she didn't want it to happen. No offense, William.

After awhile, she determined that I would never part with her, and it became a useless threat. She learned pretty quickly! What can I say? I was a sucker for my *Divatiel*!

If she was in a good mood, that alone could easily [illegible] [illegible] or [illegible] over [illegible] her head so [illegible] [illegible]. A little [illegible] [illegible] the nape of the neck. [illegible] and [illegible] [illegible] I had other [illegible] [illegible] I had only [illegible] [illegible] and that was [illegible].

[illegible] I was busy [illegible] [illegible] either sit on my [illegible] [illegible] [illegible] [illegible] [illegible]

[illegible]

[illegible] [illegible] would [illegible]

[illegible] [illegible] [illegible] [illegible] [illegible] [illegible] [illegible] [illegible]

[illegible] [illegible] her head [illegible] [illegible] [illegible] [illegible] [illegible] [illegible] and [illegible] [illegible] [illegible] [illegible]

[illegible] [illegible] when [illegible] I thought [illegible] going to send [illegible] back to [illegible] [illegible] [illegible] expression [illegible] her face [illegible] [illegible] [illegible] of her head. She [illegible] [illegible] and it [illegible] [illegible].

After a [illegible] she [illegible] that [illegible] with her [illegible] [illegible] [illegible]

Chapter Seven

Laying and molting

After another trip away, I came home, expecting to see Jaké sitting on her perch in her cage. I walked in, looked to the counter – and she wasn't there! Now, her cage was there, the door was closed, but she wasn't in sight.

I was petrified! In a panic, I started to look around the house. I called my co-worker who had been taking care of her.

"She was fine this morning," she said.

Well, then, where the heck is she?!! I thought.

I heard a rustling, and Jaké appeared out of nowhere, climbing onto her perch. I realized that she had chewed a corner of the newspaper that lined the cage bottom, and crawled under it. No wonder I couldn't see her!

She was making funny noises and doing a sort of dance that I thought was a *Happy Dance* now that I was home. I was proud of my little girl for being so creative in my absence. She had to have something to fill her days with me away, and look how productive she had been.

I scooped her up and headed for our favorite hangout – the sofa. I put my head on the pillow, ready for a quick nap, and she snuggled under my neck. She gave me a couple of little nip-like kisses. Then I heard a grunt. I felt something, so I grabbed her and sat up. She had laid an egg! On my neck! Yep, definitely a female.

I didn't think female cockatiels could lay an egg without a male bird around, but I later found out that, if they're bonded to a human very strongly, they will lay eggs. In essence, she loved me so much she wanted to have my children. Ah, if only I could find a man so loyal and thoroughly in love with me!

I held Jaké for a bit, to make sure she was OK, then I got up and put the egg in the bottom of her cage. I thought we'd go back to napping, but immediately her motherly instincts took over. She didn't want me. She wanted to be in the cage with her egg, and once she had climbed on top of it to keep it warm, she barely budged.

When morning came, she got up, took a drink of water, and took a long look at me. Apparently, in cockatiel-land, the male bird sits on the eggs half the time.

"No, sweetie," I said. "You really don't want me sitting on your egg."

She reluctantly took the hint, and went back to her baby.

She loved me so much that her first brood was eight eggs. Octo-mom!

Jaké would lay one egg every other day or so. I had no idea how draining this was on her system, but there really isn't any way to stop it. As many vets have told me, pet birds are bred to breed. The more one bird produces, the more the offspring will produce.

I also didn't realize how hormonal she would get during this time. Whew! Look out, *Divatiel*! If I thought her hissing was bad, it was nothing compared to her biting every soft part of my anatomy, from the back of my neck to my ear lobes to my fingers. Ouch! She'd get in a hormonal rage, yelling and screaming, then just lunge into my neck with her tiny beak. It was tiny but boy could it hurt!

The one thing I did love when she was with child was the way she smelled. Some women love the smell of newborn babies. I loved the way Jaké smelled when she was having babies. I would bury my nose deep into her feathers and inhale the softest, sweetest scent. I've never smelled anything like it. I call it *Eau de Hormone*^{tm}.

Jaké sat on her eggs for about four weeks, long enough for them to hatch in the real world. When they didn't, she felt like she wasn't a good Mommy, and I was afraid she was going to suffer psychological damage. I'd take the unhatched eggs away, and she dejectedly became part of our routine again.

Sometimes, Jaké would get droppings on her eggs, so when she left her babies to eat or drink, I'd pick them up and rinse them off in the sink. On occasion, one of them would slip through my hands and fall into the garbage disposal. At first, Jaké didn't notice.

Perhaps she had several eggs in her little nest and she lost count. However, one time she was on my shoulder when it happened. She immediately started screeching, flapping her wings and biting me.

Oh, no! I've scarred her for life!

Well, not exactly. Because, when that brood was done, she'd take a short break and start the next one. And if she wasn't laying them in her cage, she found various other special places to start her family, like behind the basket on top of the cupboards or behind the microwave on the kitchen counter. If it was dark and deemed safe, it became a nest.

Needless to say, none of the eggs hatched, and thankfully, she stopped doing it after awhile.

Once her egg-laying cycle was over, Jaké was on to the next activity – molting. This was an exciting time for me because I planned to let her feathers grow out and have her actually fly.

However, ya ain't met 'crabby' unless you've spent time with Jaké while she was molting! Whew!

Jaké molted twice a year. That means that she lost her old feathers and new ones grew in. The whole process took about three weeks each time, but if you add in the crabbiness quotient, it felt a whole lot longer.

Molting is probably the messiest thing birds do, and it's perfectly natural. Feathers are everywhere, and I do mean everywhere. I can't open a box, cupboard, refrigerator, book, or drawer without a remnant of a past molt making an appearance.

It took me awhile before I understood why she was so crabby while molting. I thought, *What's the big deal?* As humans, we have hair fall out and new ones grow in all the time. How different can it be for feathers?

Well, it's significantly different. When a bird molts, each feather pushes through the skin wrapped in a protective casing with a very pointy tip. Plus, feathers are much thicker than human hair. A vet once compared it to having needles come through your skin, all over your body, twice a year. Ouch!

Once the feather came through, Jaké stepped up her preening. She needed to remove the casing and let her feathers spread out and get to work, covering and protecting her body. Cockatiels are fragile creatures, consisting of only skin, bones, a small bit of blood, and feathers – so she needed all the feathers she could get. She looked pretty disheveled during that time, so I called her "*Motley*" when she was molting.

Scratching the top of her head was particularly important during the molt, so once again, I had work to do for the Alpha Bird. It was up to me to loosen the casings on her head feathers, and I knew how much it hurt, so I tried to be super gentle.

However, sometimes I wasn't paying attention and *BAM!* There it came. Not only a bite into my thumb, but a big one, with accompanying high levels of screeching. Occasionally, she'd even fly away for a second. Couldn't blame her; I'm sure it really hurt.

I know it was a lot of work and used a lot of nutrients, but her feathers were positively beautiful. My favorites are the thin little feathers from the top of her head that curve ever so gently. Her *Divatiel* plume!

When she first started molting, I happened to be interviewing an artist for a potential magazine article. He created custom masks from feathers, and he'd done some incredible work. I guess my love for Jaké was evident as we spoke, and he said he could make a custom mask using her feathers as an art piece. He would store it in acrylic.

What a wonderful homage to my baby!

However, he needed so many feathers to make one, would I mind if he mixed her feathers with ones from other cockatiels?

What! No way! I couldn't mix the *Divatiel's* feathers with another.

I decided I'd hang onto his information, and save her feathers during every molt. I now have a shoe box full of her feathers. If only I could find the artist's contact information…

Chapter Eight

The flying Divatiel

When Jaké became flighted, it was the most beautiful sight in the world. Here was this precious creature who, for four years, had been dependent upon humans for everything. Now, with her new wing feathers, she could take flight. And take flight, she did! Aside from laying her first egg on my neck, the second most precious event in her life was flying to my shoulder for the very first time. It was a joyous experience!

At first, it was like watching a child trying to ride a bicycle with training wheels. She took just short, wobbly jaunts, mostly between her cage and me on the sofa. Eventually, she extended those to the bathroom and bedroom. The condo was pretty small – only 465 square feet – so she couldn't really go too far. It was not a matter of her using her flight just for transportation. She was now able to explore on her own terms.

One problem we had to deal with was my patio door. In order to bring in the sunshine during the day, I often lifted the blinds. Once Jaké flew, I couldn't do that anymore. She couldn't distinguish the indoors from the out, and flew into the door a couple of times, leaving an oily body image on the glass. I decided her life was worth more than the sunshine, and from that point on, I kept the blinds open but down.

As her confidence grew in her piloting abilities, so, too, did her independence. She loved me, there was no doubt, but now the relationship began to change. It no longer was about us; it became even more about her. The *Divatiel* emerged, the demands began, and I'm grateful to have been part of it. After all, I allowed it to happen. I was an enabler in the *Divatiel* days of my life.

Jaké often wanted to go nite-nite much sooner than I. Generally, I was a night owl, but Jaké tried to keep sleeping hours in tune with Mother Nature. In the winter time, that meant going to sleep really early, or as soon as I came home from work. In the summer, she'd stay up a bit later.

One day while she was exploring the condo, she came upon my shower door. It was like heaven! She could be up high as birds prefer so they can be out of reach and keep an eye on things. Plus, she was near a small window so she could get fresh air. One of the best benefits was the fact that she could see me on the sofa from her vantage point.

Once Jaké discovered the shower door, nearly every night she went there before I put her in her cage to go nite-nite. In the morning, I often let her out while I was taking a shower. She didn't like to be near the water, so she flew to the towel bar and hung out there while I finished showering and putting on my makeup.

Then came the command, "INSIDE." I needed her to calmly and quickly get into her cage so I could leave for work. If I just carried her into the kitchen on my hand or shoulder, she would fly around, attempting to make me late. I started to use "INSIDE" to get her inside the cage, and after a couple of days, she understood. She didn't like it, but at least she knew what it meant and for the most part, she cooperated.

Every visit to the vet I learned something new about cockatiels, and I was given new rules. The next two were: use a full spectrum light and a spray bottle daily.

Hmm...I wasn't raising a fern. I had a lovely four-year-old cockatiel! What was with the grow light and the spray bottle?

"She's not like other birds," the vet said.

You got that right!

"She doesn't have access to sunlight. She needs the vitamin D from the sun to create calcium so she can build strong bones and create new feathers. It's also important since she's laying eggs. She needs that calcium."

OK, so I learned that the light is a full-spectrum bulb that creates the same effect on her body as sunlight. I needed to have it on at least five hours a day. Of course, that meant that she needed to be in the area of the light in order for it to be effective. In the beginning, that was not a problem, but the longer I had her, the less time she spent in the cage. Eventually, the entire house became her cage!

But, what about the spray bottle?

"Oh, cockatiels are messy," continued the vet.

As if I hadn't noticed.

"She has a lot of dust not only from the mess she makes but from her feathers, too. When you spray her, get up real close. Clear those nostrils. The spraying will help with her red throat as well. Use the whole bottle. Get her nice and wet. Eventually, her wings will develop a natural wicking property just like ducks, so the water will roll right off her."

Turns out it was really important to spray her when she was molting, too. It softened her skin and the feather casings, easing the needle-like pain a bit.

I bought a small spray bottle, and filled it with water, just like the vet said. The next day, Jaké had just gotten up and was still in her cage when I started squirting. She immediately began yelling, climbing all over inside of the cage, anything she could do to avoid the spray. Eventually, she just gave up and sat there while I dowsed her. She was soaked and disheveled. She hated it! She just kept glaring at me, and when I was done and opened the cage door, she sat there sulking for several minutes before she even considered moving.

Oh, this is going to be fun.

Eventually, as the vet said, the water did wick off her feathers and, although she never really loved getting sprayed, she allowed it.

Jaké was never a bird who enjoyed water. If you watch birds in the wild, they love taking baths, cleaning and preening themselves in the cool liquid. Not Jaké. She didn't like to be anywhere near water, except maybe two or three times a year. So, the spray baths became a source of irritation for her, although during molting season, she was a bit more appreciative.

Somewhere early on in her residency, I taught the *Divatiel* the command, "STAY." No, she wasn't a dog, but her knowledge of the command certainly served its purpose over the years. And, it always cracked up the vet.

Jaké often hung out on top of her cage on the kitchen counter, which happened to be a mere three feet from the condo's front door. As she was flighted, I worried constantly that she would sneak out when I had the door open. I always tried to be quick when I had to use any door, but this one was so close to her lodgings that I was petrified to open it.

I looked at her one day, and in a demanding way, said, "STAY!" She did a little bob like she usually did just before she took off. I said it again, in a deeper, sterner voice. "STAY!" I kept that energy going as I opened the door and went to get my mail. When I returned, she actually was still on her cage! I was so proud of her.

"Good girl, honey. You were a good girl."

Then she gave me the *'Chirp' of understanding*, and she flew onto my shoulder.

Every time I took her to the vet, Jaké got weighed. Many birds like to sit on the big perch on top of the scale, but that scared my little girl. So, the vet put the scale on the exam table without the perch, I placed Jaké on top and gave her the command. She stayed just long enough for the scale to record her weight, then she was back on my shoulder.

The first time I did this with any vet not only endeared Jaké in their eyes, they were absolutely amazed. As far as I'm concerned, it was just the little *Divatiel* showing everyone how smart she was!

Chapter Nine

Calcium, Taco Bell and the bow

As part of Jaké's recuperation, the vet prescribed liquid calcium for me to give to her. Now, just think about it. I had to capture a flying object with an iron will, hold her against my chest, and squeeze liquid into her closed beak with a tiny syringe.

Since Jaké was so observant and picked up on every little change in my energy, whenever I prepared the calcium, she'd see it and start flying around, screaming. I'd have to wait until she tired out before I could finally catch her and hold her. I hated doing that! Then, she'd squirm constantly, all the while with her beak clamped tight. She was so tiny she only needed about a drop, but most times when I finally did get her to lick the syringe, she quickly shook her head and the liquid went all over my shirt instead of down her throat.

I got smart and started setting up the calcium when Jaké was in another room. I figured, I'd sneak up on her while she was preening on the towel bar in the bathroom, and we'd be over and done with it in a few minutes. I didn't count on her sensing what I was up to, and as soon as I got within five feet of her, she was off and running.

Then, I thought, if I explained to her what I was doing and why, maybe she'd be more cooperative. Yeah, like that was going to work. It just gave her more time to think about escape routes.

Somehow we came to an understanding as she got older. Or, I just got better at hiding the inevitable. Either way, she didn't seem to fight or fly as much as she used to when it was time for her vitamins, but she was still good at shaking her head and spitting it out.

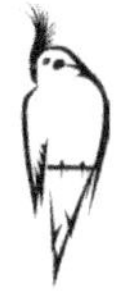

I've always been a fan of Taco Bell. Most of my adult life, I've lived within walking distance of one. Who can resist? Well, apparently, not Jaké.

One night, I came home from work, threw my Taco Bell bag on the kitchen counter, opened the cage door, and went into my bedroom to change my clothes.

I came out of the bedroom to see that Jaké was deep into my bean burrito with extra cheese and green sauce! Taco Bell used to serve up their fourth meal in a paper bag. To a cockatiel, ripping through paper with her beak was second nature. In about two minutes, she tore through the bag, the wrapper, the tortilla and into the goods.

I wasn't sure what attracted her to my dinner, but then I remembered that my vet told me cockatiels have a keen sense of smell. So, I suspect the hot sauce called to her. I was reluctant to allow her to eat my dinner, mostly because I was hungry and wanted to keep it all to myself.

Then I thought: I didn't see Taco Bell on the banned list of foods for Jaké, just avocados, and I didn't have any guacamole this time. But, I knew my vet would be none too happy for me to feed any to Jaké, especially after all the struggles she had gone through.

Maybe I can give her a little, I thought.

Visions of my vet's stern reminder flashed before me: "If you don't follow the rules, you can't come back."

I'm sure my vet had some sort of unwritten rule about Taco Bell. She read someone the riot act about pasta. And, I felt that my baby's only chance of true survival would be to keep in my vet's good stead.

I slowly pulled the burrito away, Jaké still clinging to it. She was not going to give it up without a fight! She could fly now, so wherever I went in my tiny condo, she could find me – and bite me! I finally got her onto my shoulder, thinking I could now eat in peace. However, when I opened the taco sauce to pour on the burrito, it was like she was in olfactory heaven! Her head went up, she flew around the condo, then she dive bombed me!

Jaké was too involved now. I couldn't get her back in her cage so

I could enjoy my dinner. I didn't want to eat in the bathroom with the door closed. I was at a loss. Then I noticed the blanket on the sofa. I put it over my head, scaring her away, and ate my dinner as fast as I could. When I finished and put the wrappers in the trash, there she went, right into the trash looking for what was enticing her senses. Luckily, it was only a phase. For her, not for me.

I came home from another one of my trips, so excited to see my little *Divatiel.*

"How are you, sweetie?" I asked as soon as I walked through the door. She gave me her 'Hello' chirp, and out she came. I turned around and something caught my eye. There was blood on the blinds. Lots of it. I looked further, and there was blood on the blinds on another window, too.

"Jaké, are you okay?" I asked. "What happened? Did something scare you?"

I immediately called my co-worker who had been taking care of her in my absence.

"What happened while I was gone?" I asked, panicked. "I see blood!"

"Well, I was hoping you wouldn't notice anything," she said. "I didn't know there was blood anywhere."

"WHAT HAPPENED???"

I couldn't take it anymore.

"Well, yesterday when I went to your house on my way home from work, I came in the front door, and her cage door was open. I couldn't find her. I looked around and finally found her on the floor. I must not have closed the cage door correctly and she got out."

Jaké's cage door had to be closed *just right.* Otherwise, she could kick it open. You had to sort of lift it up and to the left before latching it shut. If someone was in a hurry, chances are, it might not be done properly. And, my co-worker was always in a hurry.

I had mini-blinds on the windows, and the edges were sharp, which must have cut her when she flew into them. Birds have small amounts of blood and limited clotting ability, so bleeding can be serious.

Luckily, Jaké was fine after that incident. I cleaned up the blood, but I knew it was time for a new babysitter. I soon decided to have my vet tech watch her in my absence.

The tech's house was in the mountains and the birds she cared for were kept in an unheated cabin. I was so afraid Jaké would catch cold, but I hadn't realized all the details until I dropped her off on my way to the airport. Still, I hoped, at least, she would receive better care and attention than with the previous sitter.

Jaké was put in a room with several other birds, including a male cockatoo that screamed 24-hours-a-day for its mate, who was in an adjacent room. If I remember correctly, the female had just laid an egg and since the males are sometimes a bit too active, the egg had to be protected. Therefore, the birds were separated and the male squawked the entire time.

When I returned home from that trip, Jaké slept for three days straight. I don't think she slept a wink while I was out of town. Eventually, I either had a family member watch her, or as my travels diminished, I just spent more time at home with her. A good thing and a bad thing: I couldn't go out of the room without her freaking out, let alone out of town for a few days. She just moped…

I noticed that whenever I walked into the room where Jaké was, or even from one side of the room to the other, she would stretch her wing, first one side, then the other. I thought she was just stretching, but sometimes she seemed annoyed that I was moving around so much and she had to keep stretching over and over.

I soon found out that this is a cockatiel's way of saying, "Hello." It's like she's saying, "I see you and you come in peace." Once I knew that, then I started to say, "Hello" back to her.

Of course it was never just "Hello." It was, "Hello, baby! How is my sweetie today? Are you having a nice day? Momma loves you!" Or, something to that effect.

After a period of time, Jaké started a new thing. Every once in awhile, she'd completely bow down, and spread her wings and her tail feathers. It was incredibly beautiful when she did this, and I automatically started complimenting her on it. The vet told me that this meant, "I love you" in her language, and that it's not common for a pet cockatiel to do that, let alone on a regular basis.

Regular basis indeed. Jaké showed me she loved me two or three times a day for years.

In the midst of Jaké learning her new bow, I was getting ready for a really long trip – three weeks, 30,000 miles – and I didn't want to leave her with the tech. I was afraid it would be too overwhelming for her. So, I piled Jaké in the car and we drove to Las Vegas to leave her with my niece and *her* new little baby, a Shih Tzu.

I'd never been away from Jaké for that long, and it was heartbreaking to leave her, but I knew she was in good hands. If anyone could serve the *Divatiel* and satisfy her wishes, I knew my niece could. She's so caring and loving, it was a no-brainer to drop Jaké off in Neon City.

I also knew that my niece would let Jaké fly around. Since she'd just gotten her wings, I was certain she'd hate being cooped up for three solid weeks. And, I knew that my niece would help Jaké preen the top of her head.

When I came back from my long trip, I went straight to my niece's house to pick her up. Jaké was flying around. As soon as she saw me, she flew to my chest and spread her wings. It was like being hugged by an angel.

Chapter Ten

A pedicure and a new house

Every couple of months, it was time for a nail trim. The vet told me I would notice when Jaké's nails would be too long as they'd start to get caught in things. Sure enough, it was like it happened overnight. One day they were long but they seemed fine. The next, they got caught in everything – my t-shirts, towels, everything.

This was the first vet visit where we weren't concerned if she was actually going to live. It was a pretty routine appointment, but necessary by all means. I took Jaké into the examination room where the vet met me along with her tech. The tech had a small towel, opened the cage door and put it over my little one! It was like she was being kidnapped in the night.

When she got Jaké all together, her little head peeked out from the top of the towel, and her feet from the bottom. The tech held her across her backside while her thumb and forefinger formed a circle around her neck. It was then that I truly realized just how gentle one needs to be with a bird.

A dog or a cat you can hold with quite a bit of effort; a bird you can't. They are like a puff ball of air covered in feathers that you could crush to death very easily. Their egos and will power may be strong, and they can fly like the eagles, but their tiny bodies are extremely fragile.

I now recognized that when I needed to hold her for any reason like giving her calcium, I needed to just barely touch her. The simple act of placing my hands above her wings meant she couldn't fly, and that would keep her in place – at least for a bit. Learning how to be gentle with Jaké, I believe, helped me to become a gentler person in all aspects of my life.

Jaké, of course, squirmed and squeaked while her toes were being clipped. I had no idea how people did this on their own. I certainly couldn't. I scratched her head to remind her I was there and I spoke calmly to her. In just a few minutes, it was all over.

"Last chance to clip her wings," the vet smiled.

"No way!" I said. "She's a bird."

"OK, but take good care of her."

And I did.

After seeing how much she squirmed while the tech held her, I decided I would always be in the room for this grooming activity. She definitely was calmer with me there. It meant I had to pay for a full office visit and not a reduced grooming fee, but to me, it was well worth it.

My baby looked so beautiful! When her pedicure appointment was complete, we got back in the car, drove home and took a nap.

From the first time I brought Jaké home and she was let out of the cage, she began her search for safe hiding places. Birds don't like to be exposed. They're flighty, anxious, delicate creatures who bring great beauty into our lives. But, they also like to find safe refuges for times when they're scared. And the least little thing can scare them.

Take Jaké for instance. Something as simple as me sneezing could send her shooting up from my shoulder, zipping around in a flurry, generally crashing into something. I then had to find her and pick her up. Then everything would go back to normal. Granted, I didn't sneeze very often so it was a bit of a surprise when I did. Still, you'd think she would have gotten used to it. But, noooo! The scenario went something like this:

Sitting peacefully typing on my computer. Jaké is on my shoulder.

"Ah-choo!"

"Chiiiiirrrp!!!"

Jump. Flutter, flutter, flutter.

BAM!

"Jaké what are you doing there?"

"Chirp."

Scoop.

Sitting peacefully back at my computer. Jaké is on my shoulder.

My little condo didn't offer many hiding options. It was just under 500 square feet. We barely had room to move around. It wasn't too much of an issue, luckily, because she spent a lot of time in her cage, and we were still adjusting to life with each other. However, after four years together, things were about to change.

"Guess what, Jaké? Momma bought us a new house!"

I'd just come home from meeting with my realtor. I purchased a three bedroom home a few miles away. It was about 1500 square feet, over three times the size of our little condo. I was excited, but Jaké seemed a bit perplexed.

We sat down on our favorite sofa and I scratched her head as I spoke.

"It's so beautiful, Jaké! You're going to love it! Momma and Jaké are going to move there together. You'll have lots of room to fly around and there's a bit more counter space for you, too. Aren't you excited?"

Jaké did her normal *'Chirp' of understanding*, then looked at me with concern on her face, as if she truly did understand something new was afoot.

I got up, placed her back on top of her cage, and started making plans for the big move.

Jaké became very anxious as box after box was loaded, sealed and labeled. We didn't have much room in our little place to begin with, so filling it up with boxes just added to our cramped quarters. I tried to keep things as normal as possible for Jaké's sake, but I could see it was taking its toll.

"Don't worry, baby, it will be okay. I promise!" She'd just look at me, fear in her eyes. I knew she was confused, but once we moved, everything would make sense. Plus, she'd have a huge house to explore!

The big day finally came, and the first thing I moved was my precious cargo. I put Jaké's cage on the kitchen counter at our new home while I moved back and forth for several hours. Every time I saw her, I reminded her that this was our new house, and I'd be there soon.

When night time came, the move was done. I turned on the television, took Jaké out of her cage, lay down on the sofa and we took a nap. All was well in *Divatieldom.*

Slightly Bigger House

Chapter Eleven

The birth of the Divatiel

It was hard to leave our little condo, the place where we first met, where Jaké took her first flight and laid her first egg. Unfortunately, I only had those memories recorded in my heart. Jaké was quite camera-shy, particularly once she became flighted. As soon as I took the scary black camera out of its case, off she went and I reluctantly put the camera away. So, I had nearly zero photos of her early years in our first home. As luck would have it, she wouldn't be any more picture-friendly in our second home, but we were definitely ready for more room.

The new house was a 1,500 square foot L-shaped rancher, with the living areas facing the street, and the bedrooms and guest bath flanking a long hallway. It was built in the 1960's and hadn't been updated since. The previous few years it had been a rental property. Needless to say, the entire house needed renovating.

Moving was going to be enough of an adventure with Jaké, so I wanted to lessen the strain of the remodeling. In the three weeks before we even moved in, contractors painted, carpeted, tiled, installed new windows and even refinished the master bathroom. The only two rooms of the house untouched were the guest bath and the kitchen. Surprisingly, most of this work was done while I was out of town celebrating my parent's 60th wedding anniversary and Jaké was with my vet tech.

Once moving day was over, it was time to get settled. Jaké was particularly ready for a little more freedom, and she needed to find places where she felt safe and comfortable. The kitchen cupboards in this house went up to the ceiling like in the condo, so she couldn't claim a perch on high. However, she snooped and snooped until she found her spot.

Jaké was always an inquisitive sort, so it didn't surprise me that once out of the cage she took opportunities to explore her new surroundings. Her cage, once again, took up prime counter space in the kitchen but that didn't dissuade her from claiming even more territory – the space behind the microwave oven!

It was funny how she liked to espy from afar. Well, at least what she felt was afar. This house was so old that it didn't have a built-in microwave, so I purchased a counter-top version to place on an angle across a corner near the sink. I didn't realize I'd left just enough room for her to sneak in behind it, a deep, dark space that she was always searching for.

Jaké soon discovered it was the perfect place to hang out. She could easily play there for hours, and sneak forward just enough to have her little eye peek out to check on her environment and to see what Mommy was doing. It was the cutest thing to see this little plume of feathers and a tiny dark eye peek out from the edge of the microwave, then disappear once again.

I preferred her to be behind the microwave rather than to try to hide behind the refrigerator – another deep, dark place that also intrigued her – but it still amazed me how quickly she scouted her hideouts, then guarded them with her life. I made sure she was out of her cave whenever I used the microwave for fear she'd become a glow-in-the-dark cockatiel, and she hated when I made her move.

It was her space and from her perspective, I didn't seem to understand. The princess hissed and screeched at me whenever I disturbed her. And, as soon as she heard the 'ding' of the microwave, she flew back to the counter and scooted her way into her cave.

For the first time, I realized that she walked backwards! Sure, she could easily stroll forward. But, when it came time to go behind the microwave, she didn't walk in head first. Instead, she turned her body around and scooted in, tail feathers first! Maybe it was a natural protection mechanism for her to keep an eye on her enemies while finding refuge in her lair.

As time went on, Jaké also used the space behind the microwave as her nesting grounds whenever she decided to have babies. Any paper product – newspaper, paper towel, mail, whatever – that I placed on the counter soon became a pile of shreds as her beak tore through it and she built a soft, comfy place to protect her eggs.

Knowing how much the laying process depleted her body of nutrients, I was torn between keeping her nest clean to discourage her from laying, or providing her with more paper. It seemed she became hormonal no matter what I did, so I just went along with nature and provided supplemental nutrients. Plus, based on our visits to the vet, she was eating the best food she possibly could at the time. All I could do was let nature take its course.

The whole setup strengthened her confidence, and increased her independence. I truly believe it was at the house in San Jose where the *Divatiel* was born!

The house was so much larger than the condo, I needed to place a number of night lights around so I could find my way during the night. I also noticed that Jaké got really scared when it was too dark. She needed to be able to see, too. However, I had no idea night lights could present a problem.

During the day, Jaké was either with me, near her cage eating or behind the microwave. When it was nite-nite time, however, she was back in her cage and atop my bureau. I soon discovered that ill-placed night lights created a huge shadow of her on the wall behind or beside her cage, something that scared her nearly to death. She would see the image and didn't realize it was just her own shadow. She thought a big bird was coming to attack her in the night, and she screamed and batted about her cage until I fixed it. I had to move the night light to several different outlets until I found one that kept the big, bad shadow bird away yet provided enough light to see.

Chapter Twelve
The recliner

"Jaké, look what Momma bought!"

Now that we had more room, we also needed more furniture and a bit of a change in our routine. One day, I went shopping with a friend and found a great deal on a recliner. I'd never had a recliner before, but it seemed like the perfect addition to our new home.

At first, Jaké was a bit reluctant to go near it. The chair was new and big and, although it was a soft blue tweed, it was scary to her.

"Come on, Jaké. Let's take a nap in our new recliner," I coaxed.

I picked Jaké up on my hand and put her on my shoulder. As I got closer to the recliner, she got scared and flew back to her cage and screamed at me. For someone who liked to take naps as much as I did, and who loved to spend so much of her waking moments with me, I was taken aback. I thought she'd just accept the new chair, but I could see this was going to be a process. Still, I needed a nap and if she wanted to be with me, she'd have to get used to it.

I tried one more time, keeping her on my hand as I sat down. She jumped on my shoulder, brushing against the soft fabric, then flew back onto her cage where she yelled at me once again.

"Okay, Jaké. Momma's gonna take a nap. If you want to be with me, you'll have to come here."

I settled into my new chair, turned on the T.V. and popped up the footrest. Jaké kept an eye on what was happening, and I could tell she wanted to be part of the action, even if that action was napping. In a few minutes she flew to my leg, then climbed up my body to settle in on my shoulder. When the recliner was tilted all the way back, it was almost like being on the sofa. A few minutes more and we were both fast asleep. We had found our new favorite chair.

As time went on, napping continued to be part of our daily routine. I'd just say the magic words, and happiness would ensue.

"Jaké, Momma's gonna take a nap."

Whoosh!

Off she'd fly to the chair. Not like she didn't nap all day, anyway. There was just something special about nap time with Mommy.

Well, maybe from her perspective, but not always from mine. Sure, she was cute as a button, curled up on my shoulder, snoring away. OK, well, maybe axe the snoring part. But, she did make a little grindy sound when she was falling asleep. I'm not quite sure what it was, but it's common among cockatiels.

The grindy sound was nothing. However, she often slept facing away from me, which meant her tail feathers were in my face. Every time she or I would breathe, the feathers tickle, tickle, tickled – my nose, my eye, my lips, my chin, my neck. Wherever the feathers were, they tickled. If I nudged her to move, she went into her *Spawn of Satan* mode, hissing at me for disturbing *her* nap. Never a worry about mine.

Other times, we'd be asleep for about an hour, TV blaring in the background, totally oblivious to anything around us. The phone could ring, the sun could set, yet we both got a restful bit of sleep. Those were the best of times, but since the recliner was also the TV watching chair, Jaké occasionally got confused as to what we were supposed to be doing.

And, sometimes, she just wasn't in the mood to nap. So, she pretended it was TV time, and worked her way to any possible place that might allow my hand to scratch her head. If I was too tired to lift a finger, she would nibble on anything that she either found interesting or knew would annoy me to the point that I'd finally give in and scratch her head – buttons, snaps, threads, zippers, anything. Naptime was an all-encompassing word to Jaké so no matter how tired I was, she got to nap her own way.

Jaké was now eight years old, though she didn't look a day over two. She was young and energetic, sometimes almost too much for me to handle. Now that she had more freedom, she also became more demanding.

In addition, something else had changed in our lives. I was now consulting and working from home. I had quit my job two years previous, and I traveled a lot less as a result. Jaké got used to me spending hours upon hours with her and she relished the attention and bonding.

My home office was in the back room next to the master bedroom. I had a great setup with a corner desk, file cabinet and bookshelves. My desk overlooked the window to the backyard. Jaké often walked the long hallway with me, hitching a ride on my shoulder. Once in my office, she had a slew of options to entertain herself.

If she was content, she'd nestle under my hair and take a nap on my shoulder or preen me. Other times, she'd slide down my back and nap or preen on the top of the chair. When she was really annoyed with me, she flew to the ground and hopped onto one of the chair rungs, where she'd nap and preen for hours. She'd want to be near me, but not with me. Closeness was a word left to Jaké's definition at whim.

If I had to move the chair, she'd yell and scream at me for disturbing her peace. I also had to check the floor before I moved the chair just to make sure she hadn't hopped off. Her feet were so quiet I couldn't hear her on the ground, and the last thing I wanted to do was run her over.

If she was in a more playful mood, it was nearly impossible to get work done. She'd walk across my keyboard, pecking at my fingers to scratch her head. Or, she'd try to pry the keycaps off the keyboard with her beak which she successfully accomplished a couple of times.

When Jaké wanted attention, it didn't matter what *I* needed to do. But, if I didn't work, how could I pay the bills and buy the princess her gourmet food? She hated when I talked on the phone. She'd try to bite it right out of my hand. When she couldn't get me to put it down, she would yell – right into the receiver! Now, it's one thing for the family to hear it, but when you're on the phone with a client, it's really hard to excuse! Of course, the second I put the phone down, Jaké felt she had accomplished her task of getting my attention, and proceeded to put her head down for me to scratch.

Paper was always her downfall. I'd have files spread across my desk and every one of them wound up with at least one beak bite. She was attracted to shiny objects as well, so a paper clip or a staple set her to task. I wasn't as concerned about the paper clips as they were half her size, but the staples worried me. It was as if she could spy a stapled paper from 20 feet! It would be peeking out from under a stack and before I knew it, she had ripped a hole in it to get the staple out. I had to be quick to grab it from her for fear she'd swallow it, and in the trash it went. The staple, not the paper. I always recycle.

Another dangerous spot was the bookshelves. She often hung out on the bookshelves because she could be higher up and keep an eye on things while I was working. Books are made of what else – paper – and I'm an avid reader, so my bookshelves were quite full.

One day I was so involved in my project that I wasn't paying a lot of attention to what Jaké was doing. Big mistake! When I finished, I turned around to find she had shredded half a book! She was so proud of herself. She just sat there in the soft pile of paper, planning to use the bookshelf as an alternative nest should the microwave thing not work out.

I was so mad, but mostly at myself. It wasn't her fault. She was just doing what came naturally. I donated that book to the Jaké entertainment fund and cleared the rest of them from that shelf. She soon found comfort there and spent many hours hanging out while I worked.

There were times when she would stay in the kitchen while I made my way to my office. She would discover my absence and start screaming for me to come and get her. I refused!

"Jaké, Momma's in her office."

"Screech!"

Come and get me. You know I like to be served!

"Jaké, Momma's working. You know where my office is. Come here. You're a big girl. You can do it."

And, sure enough, she did. She'd fly from her cage, turn the sharp corner and make the trek down the long hallway to land on my shoulder. All by herself.

When she landed on my shoulder, she was winded! Now, she was a bird. She'd been flying for nearly four years. Still, I didn't realize she needed to build up her cardio just like humans do. Back and forth, up and down the hallway, she'd follow me, then rest for about five minutes until she caught her breath. After a few weeks, she eventually built up her stamina and could zip all around the house like a lightning bolt!

She was good at flying to me in my office, but she decided she didn't like the reverse commute. When it was time to head back to the kitchen, she hopped on the Mommy limo and got a first class seat.

Of course, Jaké's newfound freedom raised a few concerns. Most houses in California – and Nevada – don't have screen doors. The front doors are the only things separating an agile little birdie from a universe of freedom.

While I had taught Jaké the command "STAY," I still worried every time the door opened, even if I knew she was locked in her cage. This was a bigger place than our condo, but when you can fly as fast as a cockatiel, it doesn't matter how many extra feet there are between the cage and the front door. It's all just a matter of seconds.

The patio door was an issue as well. I used the sliding door to get fresh fruit and vegetables from the backyard. Jaké loved the new recliner so much that she often just hung out on the chair even if we weren't napping. I'm sure the softness of the fabric was comfy on her little feet.

Luckily, my little baby was scared of the front door and never went near it, no matter where we lived. The patio door she ignored as long as the vertical blinds were pulled across it, even if the blinds were opened. Still, as much as I enjoyed Jaké's ability to be a real bird and fly, I worried every single day of her life that she might somehow, by accident, slip away.

Chapter Thirteen

The traveling Divatiel

In the beginning, Jaké associated car-car bye-bye with trips to the vet. That seemed to be the only place we went by car until she got past her initial physical struggles. Once that was over, I was traveling a lot so any vehicle rides meant I was heading out of town and she was going to the sitter. In both cases, riding in the car had a negative connotation.

Eventually, that changed. Once I started my own company, I was home more often. My niece was living in Las Vegas, so the incentive to visit was quite high. Two or three times a year we'd make the trek over the mountains and through the desert, to Neon City we'd go.

"Come on, Jaké. INSIDE."

"INSIDE" was never a good thing to Jaké. It meant either I was going out or Jaké was going to the sitter or the vet. She was so spoiled with all the freedom she had now that I spent so much time at home, going "INSIDE" wasn't on her list of favorite activities.

"Jaké, we're going car-car bye-bye. We're going to Las Vegas! Do you know how many people like to go to Vegas? Well, you're one of the lucky ones."

All smiles and calm demeanor didn't make Jaké any happier. "INSIDE" was still "INSIDE," and she had no idea what Las Vegas was, or that it meant a 10 hour drive.

I loaded up the trunk with my luggage, put Jaké's cage on the front seat, and off we went. At first, Jaké was quite skittish, nothing new when it came to her personality. Over time, however, she became more comfortable with the long drive and actually was in control of the situation.

As long as the car was moving and the road was smooth, we were in birdie heaven. She'd preen, look out the window, eat, sleep and just enjoy her surroundings. She was actually quite pleasant during those moments. I'm not sure how hard it is for a bird to eat at 65 mph, but Jaké pulled it off, no problem. It was also interesting to see her balance on one little leg while preening, all the while the countryside zipping by outside.

However, as I'm sure you've come to expect with Jaké, it didn't take much to set her off. If the road got bumpy, she yelled. I'm guessing that had to do with her early life earthquake experience. If the radio was too loud, she yelled. If we stopped at a traffic light or a stop sign, she yelled. If the car fan was blowing on her, she yelled. If I wasn't paying attention to her, she yelled. If the sun was shining in her eyes, she yelled. If I had to stop to get gas, she yelled. No matter how much I explained what was going on, she wanted her life to be perfect, and if it wasn't, she yelled! Needless to say, those long drives often seemed much longer with all her yelling.

Trucks were like big, scary monsters at first. We'd be cruising along the freeway when a truck would pass. I'm not sure whether it was the size of the truck that scared her or the fact that it blocked the blazing sun and produced a big shadow. Whatever it was, it freaked her out! After a few trips and many explanations, she started to look up at the truck drivers as they passed. Eventually, she thought it was pretty cool when they went by.

Occasionally, I didn't want to make the 10 hour drive so I'd fly. At first, I left Jaké with a sitter, but when I heard that I could take her on the airplane as my carry-on, I decided to give it a try. I bought a cat carrier to put her in for the trip. Getting her inside the carrier almost made me leave her behind. Can you blame her? But, once inside, I felt she'd be just fine. This, of course, was many years ago before carry-on restrictions became so tight.

We got to airport security, and they wanted me to open the carrier. Right there. In the middle of the airport. I looked at the security guard and informed him that she was flighted.

"Her wings aren't clipped! If I take her out, I'll never see her again!"

Luckily, the guard took her to the side, looked very closely through the openings of the carrier, and determined all was well.

Once on the plane, I had to put Jaké's carrier under the seat for takeoff. I looked down, and there was my frightened little baby, giving me the *Evil Eye* through an open slit in the top. I felt so sorry for her, but I knew that once we got to my niece's house, all would be well.

After takeoff, I lifted her from the floor onto my seatback tray. The entire flight she was quiet, with her occasionally pacing, but mostly just watching me intently.

Pace, pace, glare. Pace, pace, glare.

She didn't eat or drink, and I was worried about stressing her out too much or becoming dehydrated. For landing, back under the seat she went.

As we exited the plane, she gave a couple of "Thank You!" tweets to the pilot, then off we went to meet my niece. I had my niece hold the carrier while I ran into the restroom before we went to pick up my luggage. The second I was out of sight, Jaké began to scream as if she were being attacked by big, giant bears! The lungs on that bird!

My niece brought her into the restroom and Jaké's screams echoed so loudly that even I was scared! I was certain they could be heard throughout the terminal and security would be coming in seconds. However, as soon as I came out of the stall and she saw me, she was completely quiet once again.

I bought a second cage to keep in Las Vegas so we could fly more often and I wouldn't have to pack hers for every trip. She didn't like it as well as her original cage, but she accepted it for those short stays.

Jaké adapted surprisingly well to Las Vegas. My niece had a dog, Megan, a Shih-Tzu, who luckily was as much a princess as Jaké. They became fast friends as each had a servant/Mommy who treated them like royalty.

I had read about dogs and their fascination with birds, so I was concerned at first when Jaké was out of the cage. Thankfully, royalty treat teach other with an air of aloofness and know exactly how to handle every situation. Initially, Megan was fascinated with Jaké, but she adhered to the princess creed and let her do her own thing. She was actually fine when Jaké accidentally landed on her back while she was flying. And, when Jaké would walk around the floor, Megan might sniff her, but otherwise, she just let her be.

My favorite activity for the two princesses was laps. No, not sitting in ours, but actually running laps. The house had an open floorplan connecting the kitchen, living room, dining room and family room in a circle. Jaké would fly laps around the circle while Megan followed her on the ground, often wondering what all the fuss was about.

Eventually, they'd both realize that the best place they could be was with their Mommys, and that's exactly where they went, Megan cuddled in my niece's lap, Jaké sound asleep on my shoulder. Life was good when the princesses were happy!

It was great for us to get away every now and then, but in the end, there's no place like home!

Chapter Fourteen

Communicating with the Divatiel

People always asked me, "Does she talk?" The truth is, no, but she understood a whole lot. If in fact she had the brain power of a two-year-old child, as I've heard, then two-year-old children understand a whole lot more than we give them credit for.

Teaching a bird to talk takes a lot of time, effort and consistency. You should probably also start when the bird is just a little baby. Jaké was four-years-old when she moved in, and with all the traveling I was doing, I never really had the quality time to teach her.

Now, just because she didn't talk doesn't mean she didn't understand. In fact, Jaké certainly communicated with me in her own way. She had different chirps, and she understood nearly everything I told her. So, when someone calls you a bird-brain, take it as a compliment!

Just like a mother and her newborn baby have to develop a system of communication, so did I with Jaké. A mother knows when the baby is hungry, when she needs her diaper changed and when she needs a nap. A quick peek at the clock and the look on the baby's crying face, and Mom knows exactly what she needs.

Same with Jaké and me. If she was standing on top of her cage screaming and there weren't any treats, she wanted treats. If it was about 8:30 p.m. and she let out a few chirps at the top of her lungs, it was time to go nite-nite. If it was 3:30 in the afternoon and we weren't in the kitchen, it was lunchtime and I'd better take her there in a hurry.

When Jaké became part of my family, the nite-nite screech was probably the first one I learned really well. Initially, she slept inside her cage, so when it was nite-nite time, she'd climb inside, cuddle up in one corner on her upper perch, and screech! After she screeched my ears off for a few days, I got the message. I'd close her cage door and take her to her nite-nite spot in my bedroom. There, she was perfectly quiet until the next morning when I woke up.

As time went on, Jaké spent more and more time out of the cage, so when it was nite-nite time, she could be anywhere in the house. Oftentimes, she was on my knee and I was scratching her head. When that nite-nite alarm went off inside of her, she stopped whatever she was doing, stood erect, and let out a blood curdling screech. It's as if something inside told her, in no uncertain terms, "Put your pajamas on, brush your teeth, and go to bed NOW!" If children were so intuitively trained for nite-nite, I might actually have one.

When I heard that screech, I had approximately 30 seconds to get her to bed before the screeches became louder and more frequent, like an electronic travel alarm. At 60 seconds, she'd had it. If I don't put her nite-nite, she did it herself.

Jaké had this one particular screech that was similar to the nite-nite screech, but just a little different, and often more irritating. It meant, "I don't like what's happening."

Now, to Jaké, that could be as simple as me moving my head, but for the most part, she reserved it for things such as: the television was too loud, the gardener was making too much noise, I hadn't fed her yet, I moved something where I shouldn't have, and on and on.

If I picked her up after one of my many travels out of town, I got "*the lecture*" all the way home. "Why did you leave me so long? Have you no care or concern about my well-being? No one knows my demands as well as you do, and I don't like to be ignored. Did you miss me at all? Do you even still love me? I can't believe you can bear to be away from me even for a minute, and there you go, out of town for days on end. You're lucky I'm even talking to you!"

Of course, it sounded more like, "Chirp chirp chirp. CHIRRRRPPPP! Chirp. Chirp. Chirpety chirp. Screech!!! Chirp, chirp chirp chirp. Chiiiirp!" But, you get the picture.

Jaké was so attached to me, that she really did take it personally whenever I was away, even if just for a long day. When I returned home, she'd often go to the opposite side of the cage to be as far away from me as possible, turn around, show me her butt feathers, and not even look at me! I had to tell her how much I loved her and missed her, and how sorry I was that I left her for so long and that I'd try not to do it again anytime soon. Then, she reluctantly gave in and let me scratch her head.

She loved turning around and showing you her butt feathers when she was mad. She did that at the vet one time. The tech said something to her, and she immediately spun around and chirped at me, like, "Did you hear what she just said? Can you believe it? I hope you don't agree with her because I think it was very rude of her to say that."

We laughed, but you could tell Jaké was very serious. Then I got "*the lecture*" all the way home…

Jaké also had a bit of native cockatiel in her. In the wild, when the partners are separated, they call to one another, until they can see each other once again. Jaké did this constantly when she couldn't see me. And, if I didn't respond, she flew recon until she found me. Even if I responded, she didn't stop her calls until she saw me again. Yep, she was my baby!

Although Jaké chirped rather than spoke, she understood many words. I generally treated her like a baby from day one, and I spoke to her like a toddler. Surprisingly, she understood so much of what I was saying. "STAY" was the first word that really had an impact, but "INSIDE" and "Momma loves you" were also high on the list.

Since cockatiels have the brain power of a two-year-old child, I often thought in terms of what words a child of that age would understand, and used those over and over. Office, bedroom, bathroom, kitchen, nite-nite, inside, nap, love, work, miss, hungry, thirsty, eat, drink, watch T.V., scratch your head, and so on are words Jaké easily understood. It's the same principle if you're traveling in a foreign country. You'll learn the simple, common words first and if the natives are smart, they'll use simple words when speaking back to you. It's an easy way to conquer the basics of the language.

I did speak to Jaké in sentences, but again, I used the same words over and over so she could put them in context. I used visuals, too. No, not PowerPoints or flash cards, but I would walk her around to the area I was talking about so she could get a good look. Take, for example, my new office in our new home. Over and over I walked down that hallway with Jaké on my shoulder, so she could find her way there when I'd call and say I was in my office. I'd do the same thing when I was in my bedroom. It didn't take her long to understand the different words and she always went to the correct room whenever I told her where I was.

Birds are creatures of habit and hate to have anything – and I do mean anything – change. In our case, we moved so often that as soon as Jaké saw me shifting stuff around or cleaning out boxes, she thought we were off to a new abode. Her anxiety level went up and she started screeching and flying around, always on edge, and the least little thing would set her off. I learned that speaking with her calmly and explaining the activity helped to allay her fears.

If I was rearranging a room, I'd walk her through the room on my shoulder, and tell her everything was OK. Then, I'd explain to her what I was doing. She usually picked up on my energy and emotions regardless of what I was doing, so I tried to explain things in a very upbeat way.

"Momma is cleaning out all her junk to make this a really pretty place for Jaké and Mommy." "Momma went shopping and I have to put away the things I bought." "Momma is moving the sofa over here and the book case over there, so don't be scared. I just want you to see what I'm doing. It will be really pretty when it's done."

If I went through this process, she surprisingly understood and didn't freak out like she normally would have. In fact, I would even ask her opinion on potential room colors once she knew what I was doing. I'd put paint chips on the wall and, while she sat on my shoulder, I'd point to each one and ask her opinion. She would sit there with no reaction, turn around and show me her butt feathers, or give me a chirp or a screech. That was the one she liked.

In the beginning, when I left the house, I simply said, "See ya later!" But, somewhere along the line I had read in an article that pets like to know where you're going and how long you'll be gone. One particular pet owner counted how many hours she was going to be away, so her dog could be prepared.

I thought, *What an interesting concept! I'm going to try that with Jaké.*

At first, I felt a little weird counting to 10 on work days, representing the 10 hours I'd be out, and Jaké was initially confused. However, after a couple of weeks, she seemed to understand why I counted to her every time I left the house. As the *Divatiel* didn't like to be alone, I'd get a whimper right about when I hit six or seven. And, if I counted up to 12, she almost looked depressed. It was rough on me, too, I told her but she didn't want to hear it. In fact, she got mad if I didn't count, but it became such a habit I wouldn't think of leaving home without doing it.

So, here's a little example of what I'd say when I left the house:

> *Okay, honey, Momma's going to a meeting today. I'll be gone for 1-2-3-4-5 hours. I left the T.V. and the lights on for you. Make sure you eat and drink, and stay in the kitchen. Watch T.V. and watch the house. You can even take a little nap. I'll be home as quickly as I can. Momma loves you! Be a good girl! Momma misses you!*

On occasion, I'd come home and she'd be sitting on the ottoman in front of the television, just as I suggested.

Counting the hours is one thing, but when I was going out of town and I had to count the days – yikes! Sometimes she just flew away from me into the bathroom, her safety zone. She had her independent moments, but for the most part, heaven to her was when she was with me.

When I walked through the door from the garage, and let her know I was home, I'd get one of her nice, welcome home, chirps.

If I was the least bit late, I'd get "*the lecture*" again. So, word to the wise: be as accurate in your counting as you can!

And, heaven forbid, if I forgot to tell her that the gardener was coming or that someone was going to stop by and drop something off. Oh my gosh!

"Chirp! Chirp! Chirp! Chirp! Screeeeech!" Here came "*the lecture*." It seemed to go on forever.

When Jaké greeted me like this, I had to look around to see what the issue was. There were usually tell-tale signs of the circumstances. Then came the apology.

"I'm sorry, honey. I didn't know anyone was coming over."

"Chirp."

"Really, I didn't. If I'd known, I would have told you. You know that. Momma always tells you, but sometimes I just don't know when the gardener will be here. But, Momma's home now and everything's okay."

"Chiiirp."

Then, her head went down and it was time for me to start scratching.

Jaké also had the *Evil Eye*. I could be doing something perfectly normal, and she'd just stare at me. She would tilt her head so I could only see one eye, and she'd just glare. I guess I was supposed to know what was wrong.

Sometimes the *Evil Eye* was accompanied by a tilt of the head to indicate a concern either on the ceiling or the floor. She noticed more bugs than I ever would have! It also indicated that something was invading her space.

The *Evil Eye* could also be accompanied by a rise in her plume. When the plume went up, I knew I'd better figure out what was wrong quickly, or it would soon be followed by "*the lecture*," a dive bomb or a screech!

Chapter Fifteen

Decorating her cage

To most of us, our home is our castle, and Jaké was no different.

In the early days, Jaké spent most of each day in her cage except for those few hours that I was home and allowed her some freedom. So, you can imagine how scary and emotionally painful it would be to go without it for a few days.

The cage that William gave me was brass plated, and over time, it seemed to be rusting. I didn't think it was a good idea for her to be nibbling on the rust, so I immediately started to search for a new cage. There were tall ones, short ones, wide ones, peaked ones, all sorts of cages, but none had the exact same characteristics that Jaké loved.

Her home had a flat top, so she could easily walk from side to side on it. And, it was a great place to put her treats. It also had a large door that opened, so she could hang out there when she wanted to. And, it was low enough that she could easily climb up on her way inside. She was a creature of habit, so it was really important to locate a cage that was nearly identical to the one she currently had.

I looked everywhere, to no avail. Now, at the time, you must realize that the Internet wasn't as built out as it is today. There were some items available online, but for the most part, you telephoned a company and they mailed you a catalog. Not emailed. Mailed. I also checked with my vet and looked through her catalogs, but I couldn't find anything to match the cage Jaké had.

As time went on, the cage just kept getting rustier and rustier. I really didn't like her living with the rust, and each day I became more and more desperate. Then, one day, a friend mentioned that there was a place nearby that would dip and powder coat the cage, making it rustproof forever. What a grand idea!

I contacted the company, and they said they could do it, no problem. It would take three days. Yikes! Jaké had never been out of her cage for that long. I had no other cage to use for those three days, just the travel carrier that she hated, but I knew that the best thing to do was to get the cage dipped. She did have a cage in Las Vegas that she wasn't particularly fond of, but it seemed like too much of a hassle to have it shipped out for the three days we would need it, only to ship it back the next time we went away for a long weekend.

Thus, the preparations began.

"Jaké, Momma needs to redecorate your cage. It's very rusty and it's not healthy for you to use it that way."

"Chirp." Head scratch.

"It's not going to be easy to get this done. Momma needs to take it away from you for three whole days. I'll take it to some people who will paint it and make it really pretty."

"Chirp." Head scratch.

"I'm going to take it down early tomorrow morning. Maybe we can get it back sooner if I take it in earlier."

"Chirp." Head scratch.

I thought she had given me the *'Chirp' of understanding*, but in reality she was just appeasing me. All she wanted was her head scratched. She totally ignored the major change that was coming her way. And, for a creature of habit, this was going to be a much bigger deal than either of us had anticipated.

I woke up early the next morning, hoping Jaké would be okay without her cage. Although she spent her time outside of the cage when I was home, whenever I was away, she was inside. So, I was a bit leery to just leave her free even for the hour or so it took me to deliver her cage to the dipper.

I decided I was going to put Jaké in her favorite traveling container – the cat carrier – for that hour. I took a deep breath, grabbed her, put her in, locked the lid, left her on the kitchen counter and took the cage to the dipper. He promised me it would be no longer than three days, and he'd call as soon as it was ready.

When I came home, Jaké was fit to be tied! I unlocked the travel carrier and she flew out, right at me, then onto the counter, lecturing me all the way. She was lost, and I felt her pain. I tried to explain to her what was happening and that it was the best for her in the long run, but she would have no part of it. She needed the comfort and safety of her cage, and I'd just taken it away.

At least during the daytime she could stay with me, but when it came time to go nite-nite, she had no idea what to do. She wasn't yet in the habit of sleeping on the shower door for the whole night, so I placed her carrier on top of my armoire, and left it open. Birds hate to be so exposed, but I didn't know what else to do. In the end, I don't think she slept for those three nights.

When I finally got the call that her cage was ready, I tried to put Jaké into the travel carrier so I could go and pick it up. She would have none of that. I crossed my fingers and left her out for the hour it took me to get her cage back.

When I returned, Jaké was hiding behind the microwave, waiting for me. What a good girl! If I had known she would be so well behaved in my absence, I would have left her out all the time. I brought the cage in, and I could see the calm come over her. She finally had her home back. The powder coated white finish was a little different than the plain brass, but it was guaranteed not to flake or rust, and that was good enough for us. And, it looked so much prettier and cleaner.

It took Jaké just a few minutes to readjust back to normal. As far as she was concerned, as long as she never had to go into the travel carrier again, she was happy. To this day, I still have that same cage, and although it has rusted just a bit at the very edges, for the most part, it's held up quite well. I don't think anyone would have thought that we'd use it for so many years, but we did.

Eventually, Jaké had the run of the house, but she still used her cage. The door was always open, and she sometimes climbed in, just for a quick nap. I also think it was a comfort thing for her. When she was feeling a bit beside herself, she could climb into her own private space.

I also spread her treats across the top, so she was always climbing up and down. And, she liked to sit on top of the cage and preen. It gave her a good vantage point to keep an eye on things.

The cage door occasionally was closed, like when I knew we were moving furniture in and out, or for some other reason that the door to the house had to be wide open for a period of time. I'd rather have her locked in her cage and not have to worry about her flying out the door.

She was also in her cage whenever we went car-car bye-bye. She liked the variety of going different places, unless of course, she was heading to the vet or to a family member's house because I was heading out of town. For the most part, she loved having the freedom of being in the cage at her discretion, not mine.

Our home may be our castle, but to Jaké, her cage was her comfort.

Chapter Sixteen

The quirky Divatiel

The older Jaké got, the stronger she seemed to be. By now, I was used to her various cycles of laying and molting, sleeping and playing, yelling and loving.

Luckily, the stronger Jaké got, the less we needed to visit the vet. I went at least once a month to buy food for her, but aside from her quarterly pedicures, Jaké only had to go once a year for a check-up. We certainly were both relieved and I am forever grateful she made it through those tough early months.

Still, I learned something new each visit to the vet.

"Are you adhering to the rules?" the vet asked.

It was the same question she asked every time I brought Jaké in for a check-up. All she had to do was take one look at Jaké to know I ran a tight ship at home. Still, the interrogation came with every visit.

"Are you feeding her fresh vegetables every day? Does she get at least 10 hours of sleep a night? Are you spraying her and using her light?"

Yes, yes and yes. I was so afraid of doing something wrong and having the vet cut me from her patient roster. But, one day, she hit me with something new.

"You're not using non-stick cookware, are you?" she asked in a sly tone.

I was taken aback. Everyone was cooking with non-stick cookware. Why would she ask me that? I started shaking.

"Uh, yes, I do. Is there a problem?"

I felt like that response should be followed by the word 'officer' but I knew better than to tease the vet too much.

"Is there a problem?" The vet was like a caged lion, ready to roar. "Is there a problem?"

Yes, that's what I asked. Do you need me to rephrase?

"You need to throw out all your non-stick cookware. No arguments."

Uh, gee, I wondered if she knew how much I'd paid for all my cookware. And, once I threw it away, how would I cook?

"What is the issue with non-stick cookware? I mean, half the world uses it."

I had to know more, even though I was ready to grab Jaké and run out the door should this discussion take a mean turn.

"The chemicals in non-stick cookware can kill a bird. Birds are sensitive to them, particularly if something is burned. So, they need to go."

Well, this was a tough one, but I wanted to do what was right for Jaké. I'd feel terrible if I was cooking dinner and suddenly she keeled over.

"I'll give them away as soon as I get home." I always liked an excuse to shop.

The vet continued her exam. "Are you burning candles?"

What's with all the questions today? All these years, and I haven't had these questions! What could be wrong with candles?

"Uh, yes, sure, I burn candles occasionally. They smell pretty."

"Well, they're bad for the bird. Not only do they bother her respiratory system, but since she's flighted, she might fly through a lit candle and start on fire."

The vet turned toward me for dramatic effect.

"And you wouldn't want that to happen now, would you?"

Ouch! Cut right to the heart. I had noticed that Jaké's nostrils turned red when I burned candles, but I really wasn't aware it could affect her that badly.

"You're right," I said apologetically. "I'll stop burning candles immediately."

The vet eyed me, trying to detect my level of conviction.

"Good. She looks great. Now, let's keep it that way."

Jaké let out her happy chirp, fluffed up her feathers, and looked up at me as if to say, "Let's blow this pop stand and get back to the castle."

"Thanks, doctor. I appreciate the education."

I picked up Jaké's cage, paid the bill and off we went, back to *Divatieldom.*

Jaké had her quirks, and just like humans, they changed over time. One that always made me laugh was how she hated to hear the sound of a utensil scraping a dish. It didn't matter where she was in the house – sometimes even sleeping in the bathroom – but as soon as she heard it, she started to yell!

The more time Jaké spent out of the cage, the more I noticed her little quirks. The first, of course, was walking around on the floor. The second was her ability to walk backwards.

When Jaké walked around on the floor, she followed me just like a loyal dog. But, if I suddenly reached my destination and decided to return to my starting point, Jaké simply walked backwards! Of course, she only did it for a bit, maybe a foot or two, before she stopped and gave me that, "Mommy, up!" look.

Once she settled on the corner behind the microwave as her cave, she often walked backward to get there. She'd fly from her cage to the counter, turn around to watch me, then waddle back into the dark. Sure, sometimes she'd walk in face first, but most of the time, she walked backward, waddling like a youngster learning to ice skate backwards for the first time.

"Jaké, Momma's boyfriend is coming over."

Jaké's eyes lit up, inquisitively. She didn't like when anyone else was here. She preferred it to be just her and me. However, Momma needed to have a life!

"Now, when he gets here, you be really nice to him, okay?"

"Chirp."

"After we have lunch, we're going to go out for a bit. You haven't met him yet, but he's a really nice guy and I want you on your best behavior, okay?"

"Chirp."

The doorbell rang and Jaké's plume shot up. She stood erect and started pacing.

"It's okay, Jaké. It's just Momma's boyfriend. STAY!"

I opened the door and in he walked, wearing a sweatshirt and a baseball cap.

Jaké went wild! She started flying all around, yelling and screaming, buzzing his back and shoulders. I thought she was just jealous because he kissed me, so I ignored it.

Jaké flew until she tired out and landed on the floor. I picked her up and held her close so I could introduce her to my boyfriend. The closer we got, the more she squirmed and at first chance, flew out of my hands and around the room again.

Then something happened.

He took his cap off.

Jaké calmed down.

I picked her up and introduced her to him, and she was just as sweet as pie! She sat on my shoulder and snuggled under my chin, chirping peacefully all during lunch.

"Wow, that's one strange bird you have there," he said.

"No, I think she's just very protective," I countered. What did I know?

When lunch was over and we were getting ready to go out, he put his cap back on. And, once again, Jaké went crazy! So, he took his cap off, and Jaké was a gem. Cap on – crazy. Cap off – calm.

"What's up with that?" he asked.

I thought about it. I'd been living in *Divatieldom* for quite some time now. I looked at her, I looked at him, I looked at the cap. I've got it!

"She thinks you're a big bird with the cap on," I said. "So, please don't wear it here anymore."

"Whatever," he scowled.

We had our date. We had several dates. He never wore the cap in the house again. We eventually broke up. But, whenever Jaké saw someone with a baseball cap, she always had the same reaction. So, no baseball caps in the house!

My baby was born in May 1989, just a few months before the 7.1 Loma Prieta earthquake in Northern California. She was with William then, so I'm not sure what city he was living in at the time. However, I went through the quake and I must admit it was pretty scary for an adult and I knew what was going on. I can't imagine what it was like for little Jaké who had no clue.

However, my intelligent little *Divatiel* took advantage of the situation – she learned to predict, or at least feel, earthquakes. She became my very own, personal USGS (U.S. Geological Survey).

For years, scientists have said that animals feel the earth's vibrations much sooner than humans or the sensitive equipment we have embedded in the earth's crust. And, I'd say, Jaké proved that to be true.

Sometimes she'd act a certain way, a different way than normal, and when I watched the news later that day, I'd find out we'd had a 3.1 or 2.9 or some other small quake that humans don't really feel. They have to be a bit bigger for us to really notice. But, a little birdie who had been through the biggest one in the area in decades, well, she noticed everything.

I got to the point where, when she acted this certain way, I'd call the USGS 24-hour recorded line. Sure enough, we'd just had a mini-quake.

Jaké, you rock! No pun intended.

When we were in the car and the road was bumpy, she often thought that was an earthquake. So, I had to explain to her that it was just the road and nothing to be worried about. Still, she usually screamed at me until the road smoothed out.

We'd been living in the house for nearly two years. My niece was still in Las Vegas, and we made several trips a year to visit her. Now, I received some good news from my sister. She was moving to Las Vegas in the summer, and my niece was getting married!

That was it. I knew I'd be traveling back and forth all the time, just to be with my family. I missed those spontaneous get-togethers and fun family events. There was only one thing to do – move to Las Vegas!

"Jaké, how does the desert sound to you?" I asked.

Cockatiels are originally from Australia, and although this one was born and raised in California, I suspect she still had some native bird in her. She could do well with the heat, especially when the air conditioning would be on so much.

Jaké just looked at me forlornly. I'm certain she thought I must be joking. We had just moved a little while ago. Heck, she had just gotten used to *flying around this house.* Now we were moving to a whole new house?

We sat on our favorite recliner and had one of our many heart-to-heart talks. I scratched her head and explained to her how wonderful it would be to live so close to family.

"Jaké, just like you love to have Momma around, Momma loves to have her family around," I said, hoping she'd understand. "I know it's a big move, and Momma is really busy right now so I have no idea when I'll have time to pack, but it will be a fun new adventure. And, you'll get to see a lot more of Megan, too!"

Jaké gave me her *'Chirp' of understanding*, although I'm sure she hoped it was all a bad dream.

Once again, out came the boxes and up went Jaké's plume. Boxes were never a good thing in her book. That meant change and change is not an acceptable word in the cockatiel vocabulary. They like consistency and routine. But, like it or not, we were heading to a new home.

In just a couple of months, we were packed and on our way to Neon City, far off in the desert. The actual moving day, Jaké spent her first night in a hotel. We'd been up packing all night, and it took the movers nearly eight hours to load the truck. Rather than attempt the 10-hour journey on zero sleep, we opted to check into a local hotel and catch some shuteye.

"Jaké, do you realize that not everyone gets to stay in such a special hotel? You are so lucky!"

I had to stay within view in order for her to be quiet, which I'm sure the neighboring rooms appreciated. The majority of the night I let Jaké out of the cage so we could relax and she understood that all was okay, but when it was time to sleep or I needed to open the door for room service, "INSIDE" she went.

The next day we drove for about five hours. Once again, overwhelmed with drowsiness, we checked into a hotel and had a good night's sleep. The following day we arrived at my sister's house to relax until the moving truck arrived.

Welcome to fabulous Las Vegas!

Oh, how Jaké hated to be on this gym! It didn't last very long in our house.
credit: Cindi R. Maciolek

Jaké was very good at giving me the *Evil Eye*, no matter where she was, even in the safety of her cage.
credit: Cindi R. Maciolek

Everyday, I gave Jaké fresh treats, and placed them on top of her cage.
credit: Cindi R. Maciolek

I loved when Jaké would sit on my shoulder and rub her head on my chin, although it tickled a lot and I hated when she did it while we were supposed to be napping! In the photo, you can also see the necklace she unhooked the first day she came home with me.
credit: Jackie Carpenter

Here's my baby, resting on the shower door where she loved to sleep or just hang out.
credit: Cindi R. Maciolek

Head scratching was a daily activity which could last for hours.
credit: Jackie Carpenter

Another favorite hangout was her basket on top of the cabinets.
credit: Cindi R. Maciolek

Jaké also loved to hide in her basket and keep an eye on things.
credit: Cindi R. Maciolek

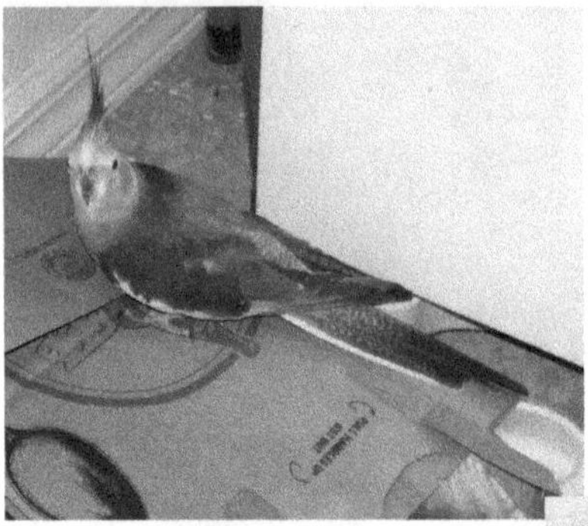

Jaké was so proud of herself when she figured out how to get past the bag and the dust-pan and make her way into the dark space alongside the refrigerator.
credit: Cindi R. Maciolek

She also had a very territorial issue at the time, and spent days attacking the dustpan!
credit: Cindi R. Maciolek

Jaké bowed for me every day to tell me she loved me.
credit: Cindi R. Maciolek

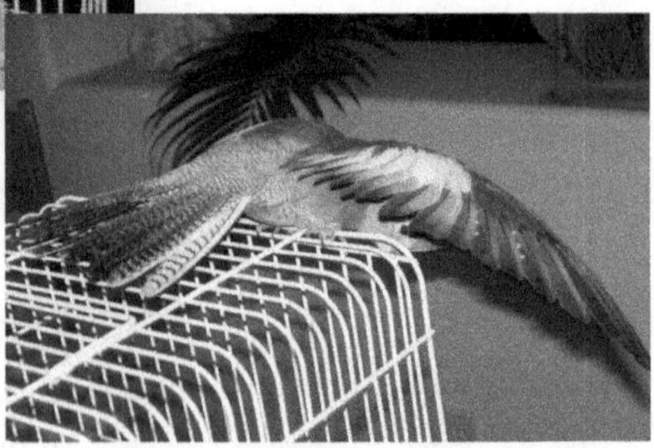

Pay Attention! Jaké made sure I was always watching her bow. You can see her eye peering out from under her wing. If I wasn't paying attention, she would bang her wing on the cage until I did.
credit: Cindi R. Maciolek

Part Two
Las Vegas, Nevada

The Great Big House

Chapter Seventeen

My baby is stuck in the cupboard

Moving to a new home meant lots of things – new rooms to learn, new routes to fly, new places to discover. Sometimes, the discovery gets the best of all of us.

Our entire time together in San Jose, we lived in single story houses. But here in this new town, I purchased a rather large 3,700 square foot two-story home. With the master bedroom and office on the first floor, I hardly ever needed to go upstairs. I was expecting that, as a bird, Jaké would find the large, open spaces, particularly at the center stairwell, to be of particular interest.

I was wrong. In fact, whenever I went near the stairwell, she would freak! She clung to me as if her life depended upon it. If she was on my shoulder and I decided to climb the stairs, she flew off into the kitchen before I reached the fifth step. I don't think she went upstairs with me but once, and that was because I held her close to my chest, trying to acclimate her. It didn't work.

What did intrigue Jaké right from the start were the kitchen cabinets. Our previous homes had soffits above the cabinets, so there wasn't any room for her to go on top.

However, this house was different. One of her favorite places to hang out became the top of the kitchen cabinets, and there were lots of them at different heights and depths for a very elegant look. She had so much fun watching me from on top, and she knew it was difficult for me to reach her up there.

The house had 12-foot ceilings, and the cabinets in the kitchen were quite tall. I never considered that they were mounted at different depths from the wall; I thought that some were just deeper than others. Silly me.

Jaké was exploring the top of the cabinets one afternoon while I was on the phone. I could hear her little contented chirps so I knew she was just fine. All of a sudden, I heard a *Whoomp*!

I looked up, and she was gone! Oh my gosh! Where did she go? It was like she was in a magic act, sent to some unknown locale. Was there a hole in the wall? Would we have to tear apart the kitchen to find her? Would I find her before she perished? Was she injured?

I started listening intently and discovered her movement near the base of one of the cabinets. There was a small piece of Masonite covering the bottom, but it appeared that there was an open space at the top. Jaké snooped into the dark space, as she liked to do, and fell right to the bottom. I tried to push up on the board, but it seemed to be in there, rock solid. I was also worried about hurting her if it snapped up too quickly, but I needed to get her out of there ASAP.

The house was in a brand new community, so the builder was still on site. I called the emergency number and begged one of the carpenters to come over. It was right at the end of the work day, and he wanted to get home to his family, but I guess my crying and screaming convinced him to come to my house before he left.

It took about 20 minutes until the carpenter knocked on my door. Until he arrived, I kept talking to Jaké, letting her know that help was on the way.

"You have to help me!" I screamed when he arrived. "My baby is stuck in the cupboards. I don't know what to do. Help me! Help me, please!"

The carpenter looked at me like I was a lunatic. How could a baby get stuck in the cupboard? He thought I meant I had a real baby stuck in a closet and I couldn't get the door open.

"No, no, here in the kitchen," I corrected him. "In the bottom of the kitchen cabinets. Listen."

He noticed Jaké's cage on the counter as we walked toward the drop zone. We both listened intently as I tapped the board gently. We could hear Jaké hiss and attempt to move.

"It's okay, baby," I said, trying to calm her nerves. "The nice carpenter is here and he's going to get you out."

I looked pleadingly at the carpenter, hoping he truly could.

I'm usually a pretty handy person, but I didn't know exactly how these boards were placed in the bottom of the cabinets. I knew he would. I didn't want to hurt Jaké but I also didn't want to damage the wood of my brand new cabinets if I could help it.

He quickly assessed the situation, went out to his truck for some tools, and in 30 seconds, Jaké came flying out of the cupboard, yelling and screaming. My baby was fine!

The carpenter tried to sneak out in all the excitement, but I wouldn't let him leave. I didn't want to risk this same thing happening again, so I made him cut pieces of Masonite for the openings on top of the cabinets right then and there. He obliged, reluctantly, and Jaké was episode free for as long as we lived there. At least as far as the kitchen cabinets were concerned!

Since that incident, every time we moved to a new house, the top of the kitchen cabinets were the first thing I checked. Sure enough, there were openings on most of them, so before I allowed Jaké to explore, I covered them up. Just as a parent wraps the sharp edges of a table, or locks the cabinet doors to prevent harm to a child, I went through preventive measures every time we moved just to ensure Jaké would be okay. I didn't know what I'd do without her.

Chapter Eighteen

The pleasures of flight

When we moved to Nevada, I thought for sure our earthquake days were over. I was wrong.

We hadn't been in our new house more than a couple of months. It was late fall 1999. Jaké was sleeping in her cage at that time, right next to my bed on a little table. She was still getting used to the house so I thought that was the best way to help her adjust.

I went to bed around 2:30 a.m. or so. I was relaxing, just about to fall asleep, when she started screeching and flapping her wings. I thought maybe she had a night fright. I got up and started talking to her calmly, explaining that everything was all right, but she just kept yelling at me.

All of a sudden, the ground started to rock and roll pretty hard. It went on for quite a few seconds. I was in shock! I didn't think Nevada had earthquakes, but my personal USGS was still hard at work. When the earthquake was over, Jaké bowed and spread her wings as if to say she was the more intelligent one. I had to agree, I bowed to her greater wisdom. She chirped and went to sleep. All was well.

As it turned out, the earthquake took place in Southern California, and it spread far and wide. I also discovered that Nevada is the third most active state for earthquakes, behind Alaska and California. I guess those mountains had to come from somewhere.

After the earthquake episode, I was excited to see how Jaké would acclimate to her new surroundings. She eventually realized that we were staying in our new abode, and she formed new routines. With the high ceilings, there was lots of room to fly, and lots of new places to hang out. Yet, life with Jaké was always an adventure.

Birds are very flighty. Go figure. As smart as Jaké was, she still got scared. And when she did, she just took off and started flying around, anywhere there was open space. In the wild, that's the entire sky. In a house, it's as far as you can go without bumping into something. She usually wound up in any number of obscure spaces and unexpected spots.

Many things scared Jaké over the years, some of which I'll never know. However, her landing places were like a treasure hunt. Cockatiels do fly extremely fast, so in a matter of seconds, she could quickly be in any room of the house.

As soon as she landed, she gave one loud chirp. I headed in that direction, but many times, I didn't see her. Her gray feathers seemed to blend in with the background like camouflage, so she didn't always stand out.

I found her on my nightstands, atop my lamps, in my bathtub, on top of the comforter, underneath the ottoman, in a pail, in a waste basket, in a basket of laundry, in the washing machine, in a plant, and on and on. Once, she landed on top of a decorative chair I had in the hallway. It was covered with ivy and had an artificial bird on top. She sat right next to the bird. It was like trying to find E.T. in the closet of stuffed animals!

She became perfectly capable of getting out of where she was, in most cases, simply by spreading her wings and flying. But, because she was scared and she was usually in a place she didn't recognize, she just sat there patiently, waiting for me to find her and tell her everything was all right. Yet, she rarely gave me a chirp beyond the first, and I had to go room to room, trying to find her, because, if she saw me, she wouldn't respond. She thought I could see her, too!

When Jaké was young, she occasionally flew into the wall, just because she had so much energy and speed. She became more controlled as she got older, but I still worried when she took off like a rocket.

If she wasn't scared but mad instead, that was another story. Cockatiels have incredible eagle eyes, and when they focus, they are extremely precise in their movements. So, on more than one occasion, Jaké buzzed me with her wingtips. *Bam*! Right across my eyes.

When we first moved to Las Vegas, I wore contact lenses, so she managed to buzz my eyes whenever she got mad. She'd usually start from atop the kitchen cabinets, buzz me, then go back on top where I couldn't reach her. She'd scream at the top of her little lungs, and buzz me again.

Oftentimes, she was just upset that I was gone for the day, or not paying enough attention to her. Whatever the reason, I decided not take any more chances and opted to wear glasses.

In addition to flying when she was scared or mad, Jaké flew with a purpose. And, therein lay the problem of having her flighted.

First came the biggest concern: the open door. The weather in California and Nevada is beautiful, and most homes don't have screen doors like they do back East. So, once a door is open, there's nothing protecting a curious bird from finding her way into the wild blue yonder.

"SHUT THE DOOR!" was heard every single time there was someone in or near a door besides me. It wasn't only that she might be attracted to the open door, but if I was anywhere near it, she may have been tempted to fly to me and somehow get caught up in a gust of wind. Knowing how she flew when she was scared, I was petrified that I'd never see her again if she mistakenly found her way outside. So, "SHUT THE DOOR!" was a common refrain.

If I knew the door would be open for a short period of time, and she wasn't safely in her cage, she generally heeded the "STAY" command. However, sometimes, just like a two-year-old child, she didn't always listen to Mom.

Also, because she was flighted, if she wasn't where she wanted to be, just by flying, she could be. And she knew this.

If I put her on the chair and she wanted to be on my shoulder, she was.

If I put her on my shoulder and she wanted to be on top of the cabinets, she was.

If I put her nite-nite and she wasn't ready, she flew to me.

If I put her on top of the refrigerator and she wanted to be in my salad, she was.

Most times, I just dealt with it. After all, I wanted her to be flighted when I got her. But, it did present problems.

For example, I didn't take Jaké into the garage when I needed something because there were too many places she could fly and I wouldn't be able to rescue her. Or, she could get hurt because it was unfamiliar territory and she wouldn't know where to land.

The good thing was that she was afraid of the garage and didn't want to go there. The bad thing was that it seemed whenever *I* needed to get something from the garage, she was always glued to my shoulder, and *I couldn't go there!* If I put her on a chair, she flew to me. No matter where I put her, she flew to me. Then, the moment I opened the garage door, she gave her scaredy-cat cry and I could feel her getting ready to take off and land in the garage abyss.

Sometimes she took advantage of her flying ability after I put her nite-nite. Generally, once she was in the bathroom and the light was out, she was fast asleep. However, once in awhile, she decided that she just wasn't ready. So, I'd be sitting in the living room or walking by the bedroom door, and *Phooomp*! She was on my shoulder.

She thought this was perfectly fine. She gave a little "Hello" chirp, cuddled up under my hair, and went to sleep.

Jaké knew I loved her and I allowed her to get away with these things. Lucky girl!

Over the years, aside from night frights, Jaké pretty much slept like a baby. And I do mean sleep. During the winter, she'd go to bed as early as 6 o'clock, and she never had a problem sleeping in. Occasionally, she'd yell for me to get her up, or fly to me in bed while I was still sleeping, but she was usually content to stay where she was until about noon.

One night in our new Las Vegas home, we were sleeping calmly, Jaké nite-nite in her cage on a table next to my bed. Behind her was a small section of wall. I went to bed at my usual late night hour, and fell fast asleep.

About an hour or so later, I heard a noise like no other.

Splat! Splat! Splat!

I was scared out of my mind. I looked over to see Jaké sitting on her perch like normal. However, there was nothing normal about the wall behind her. It was covered! As if a baby had thrown a bowl of oatmeal with a spoon!

I picked her up and cuddled her for awhile, and she seemed to be okay. My wall, on the other hand, was not. I had no idea what had happened but it just didn't look good.

There weren't any vets who specialize in birds at the 24-hour hospitals here in town, so I had to risk the rest of the night that Jaké would be okay. I gingerly put her back in her cage, and fell asleep. Not another peep came out of her until morning.

When I took her to the vet, she felt everything was just fine. It seems Jaké's crop needed cleansing, and she did it by disgorging her food onto my bedroom wall. Supposedly it's not a common event, but it does happen, and it's nothing to worry about as long as it doesn't recur.

For the next several nights, we both feared a repeat, but luckily, nothing happened. The wall regained its former luster, and Jaké regained her sleepytime crown.

Chapter Nineteen

Little things I learned about my Divatiel

Over the years, I've learned a few things about cockatiels:

First of all, they hiss. Like a snake. No, they don't have any teeth or spew venom, but they do hiss. Jaké was very good at it. Ask anyone in my family.

In fact, my niece and her family recently welcomed a cockatiel into their lives. And what did her kids say about their new bird?

"She doesn't hiss like Jaké!"

Jaké had three distinct types of hisses. The first was your typical hiss. If you went near her, made a noise she didn't like, took something away from her, or in general, just annoyed her, she did a straightforward hiss. Sometimes, it was followed by a little nibbley bite depending on how physically close you were to her.

Her second favorite hiss was when she was hormonal. She rocked back and forth, wings spread, down on her haunches ready to attack. *HISS*!

The third type is what I call a hissy-kiss. If you asked her a question and she didn't want to be disturbed, she gave you a little mini-hiss, followed by a nod of the head.

To be the recipient of a hiss, you didn't even have to be near her. If she felt in any way you were infringing on her territory or well-being, you got hissed!

Birds – well, at least Jaké – get scared and verbalize it. She was better than a watchdog. When she caught the least little movement by a person or other creature outside, she stiffened up, her plume rose, and she let out a little squeal, just like humans!

The first time I experienced it, I thought it was a quirk. Now, I realize, it was really part of who she was. She used to squeal, then fly. As she aged, she only squealed. I had to reassure her everything was OK. Otherwise, she just stared at me. She was like a little kid watching her Mom.

If Mommy's scared, then so am I. If Mommy is OK, then I'm OK, too.

Jaké was good with time. If we took a nap and I told her I needed to be up by a certain time, she woke me within a few minutes of my request, whether I stated it in terms of "four o'clock" or "thirty minutes."

She was also good at letting me know when the phone rang or if someone was at the door. If I was in the shower or blow drying my hair and I expected a phone call or a visitor, I just had to listen for Jaké to make her special noise to alert me. I tried to remind her to listen for the bell, but even if I didn't, she responded the moment she heard it.

Jaké had always been very observant. It was as if she had a photographic memory. She had the same scared reaction if anything was changed in the house. If a picture was different, a chair was moved, or something was missing, Jaké noticed. You just couldn't put anything past her.

As soon as she noticed – and it usually took approximately 10 seconds – up went her plume, her body was erect and she had that deer in the headlights look. Sometimes she let out a little, "I'm scared" noise.

Whatever the reason, I either had to change it back the way it was, or explain to her in excruciating detail why it was different and that it was okay. Just like a little kid, she looked to me, her

Mom, for reassurance. Once she concluded that the situation was acceptable, she went back to her normal behavior, with a cautious eye, just to make sure everything really was okay.

Then, there were times when the change was totally unacceptable. That's when she would fly either up to the cupboards, right at me, or around and around yelling and chirping, until she got tired and landed somewhere. When I picked her up, which I did, "*the lecture*" began.

When you live with a bird, especially one that's bonded with you, you have to expect to be part of the flock. Even though Jaké was always a domesticated bird, she often showed her instinctual nature. While I tried to teach her the ways of humans, she spent her time training me on the wild side.

If I moved away from her location, she called to me. It was my duty to call back. She continued to do that as I roamed around the house, making sure I was still within range of coming home to the nest. If she couldn't see me, when I called to her, she responded. However, if I couldn't see her and she did see me, she wouldn't respond.

I could hear her thinking, "*I'm right here, Mother.*"

But I couldn't try that attitude with *her*. After all, she was the *Divatiel.*

Jaké wandered around the house at will, and there were times I couldn't locate her. That usually meant she was sleeping somewhere. She found comfort in taking naps on the rungs of my office chair. Sometimes when I'd been out for the day, I'd find her in my office sound asleep, waiting for me to come home. You gotta love that.

Another one of her favorites was the bottom rung of the dining room chairs. If I couldn't find her anywhere else, I just had to bend low and there she was, all cuddled up and cute as a button.

My sister and her husband learned quickly that Jaké's chirps were meaningful when I let them babysit while I was out of town. My sister likes to sleep with the shutters open so the sunlight wakes her in the morning. Well, the *Divatiel* liked to sleep in. So, when the sun came streaming through the windows, Jaké went wild! My sister thought something was wrong with her. She had never heard her scream like that before.

Out of the blue, she decided to close the shutters. Then, an amazing thing happened. Jaké quit screaming! She needed a dark room in order to sleep. So, lesson learned: keep the room dark and Jaké would sleep. If only William had learned that.

Another time, Jaké was in her cage in their kitchen. My sister and her husband had fed her, so they were making their own breakfasts. Yet, every time they opened the refrigerator, Jaké let out a chirp. They couldn't figure out what was wrong until they realized they hadn't given her *her* treats! So, out came the lettuce, parsley, broccoli and cucumber, and Jaké was quiet once again.

Jaké knew her name, and generally answered to it. However, through the years, I'd given her many nicknames. Of course, I used the usual terms of endearment, like honey, sugar, pumpkin, sweetie, and so on. But, she acquired a few that were just for her.

SNOOPY: Snoop, snoop, snoop. Jaké constantly snooped. She particularly liked to find dark hiding places. It mostly related to her hormonal stages, but in general, she just liked to snoop!

CUTIE-PATOOTIE: It started out just being cutie, but I eventually added patootie to the name, and even wrote a little ditty that I sang to her.

Cutie-patootie, you're my little one.

You make the day bright like the morning sun.

Cutie-patootie, you're the one.

BABY: Of course, Jaké was my baby. There's no doubt about that. I wrote a little ditty for this one, too.

You are Momma's baby, and I love you so much.

You are Momma's baby, yeah.

Seems I wrote a lot of little ditties for her. When I was stuck for words, I simply sang:

Momma loves you, Momma loves you.

Momma loves you, Momma loves you!

Then there was the one for treats:

Fresh fruit and veggies

Fresh fruit and veggies

Fresh fruit and veggies

Making their way to you

I don't know why I sang that song since she hardly ever ate fruit, just veggies.

CHIPPY-MONKEY: This one started out as chipmunk, because she liked to run around on the ground so much. It evolved into chippy-monkey, and often was shortened to just chippy.

TWEETHEART or TWEETIE PIE: I think these are self-explanatory.

MOTLEY: When Jaké molted, she got a little shabby looking. As her feathers started growing in, her beautiful feathers were interspersed with pointy sacs housing her hard work with new feathers. Until everything filled in and the sacs were cleaned away, Motley she was!

LETTUCE BREATH: Jaké loved her treats, and lettuce, broccoli and cucumbers were her favorites. Just like garlic stays on our breath, lettuce definitely stayed on hers, at least for a bit. It seemed that after she ate her lettuce, she hissed at me from a very short distance, and I had the pleasure of smelling her lovely lettuce breath.

No matter what I called Jaké, she'll always be my little *Divatiel*!

In Las Vegas, instead of music, I usually left the television on when I wasn't home. In fact, as soon as I woke her up in the morning, she wanted the television on. I think it was a comfort thing for her. Here again, I had to be careful of the programs.

I know a lot of folks who leave the television set to *Animal Planet*, but I think that would have scared her. If I watched it personally, it might not have been so bad. But, to leave it on when I was heading out the door I think would have caused her some discomfort.

I usually set it to HGTV. It's a station I watch regularly so she was used to the tone and flow of the shows. It was just like Mom was home, only I wasn't! There's nothing scary on the station, and you don't feel the vibe of doom and gloom like you would from a detective series. So, she was okay with that.

On Saturday nights, we watched the British comedies on PBS. Jaké's ears perked up when she heard the theme song to *As Time Goes By*. I always sang it to her. We consider it "our song."

Jaké much preferred the recorded theme sung by professional artists compared to my attempts at singing it, as indicated by the nibbles and hisses I got every time I tried to serenade her. However, if she had really hated it, I probably would have gotten "*the lecture*."

Chapter Twenty

Boo-boos for my baby

I've mentioned before just what incredibly fragile creatures cockatiels are. They have beaks and feet and a small bone structure, with about enough blood to fill a thimble or so. And, only moderate clotting abilities. They weigh somewhere between three and four ounces, and most of that is feathers. Well, and ego when it came to Jaké.

As you can imagine, it's a miracle that something so precious and delicate can not only survive but have so much personality. When Jaké sank her beak into my neck, screamed into my ear or repeatedly got into things she wasn't supposed to, I completely forgot about her fragility. She may have only weighed four ounces, but when she was flying at full speed and she landed on my shoulder, I could feel it! *Wham*! Jaké had arrived.

In the grand scheme of things, all birds have a similar delicate nature, and it reminds me every time I see a wild bird that some greater power is definitely looking out for them. The other interesting characteristic about birds is that they hide when they're not feeling well, to the point that you don't know they're sick until it's almost too late. Birds hang with their flock. If you can't keep up, the flock leaves you behind.

In Jaké's case, I was part of her team. I cared for her, followed vet directions as closely as my hectic life would allow, and reminded her 100 times a day that she was loved. Still, that doesn't mean things didn't happened to her that could have taken her life. Many birds also mate for life. Thus explains my relationship with Jaké.

She allowed me to baby her, particularly when she was not feeling well. For her, that mostly meant being on my shoulder or my knee, cuddled up and sleeping. Then, once she was feeling better, she was her independent little self once again, and made sure that I knew it!

During the years we were together, we definitely developed a means of communication, particularly during the hard times. Lucky for me, I was there to take care of her when she needed me most.

From the first time Jaké came into my life, I stayed with her during every vet visit. I didn't allow her to be taken from me or taken from the examination room for any reason, even to get her nails clipped. I always paid the extra money for a full office visit just so I could be there and calm her during the process. Jaké tended to squirm when you held her, even if I was the one doing the holding. So, for her own safety, I never let her leave the room.

We were now living in Las Vegas and I didn't have the fantastic specialist I went to in California. I searched, but the closest avian vet was way across town. I found a local animal hospital where I could take her because clipping a bird's nails is generally a simple thing to do and I didn't think they could screw it up too badly. I'd gone to this animal hospital once or twice before to have her nails trimmed, and while I wasn't thrilled with the place, it would suffice until I managed to get to the avian vet.

I had an appointment, but this day, the hospital was positively swamped. The vet was busy with an emergency case and couldn't keep her appointment with me. Jaké's nails were really long and I didn't want to come back another day if I could help it. So, the tech said she would take Jaké in back to the doctor to trim her nails, and she'd be right out in a just a few minutes.

Well, a few minutes quickly passed. Then 15 minutes. I was getting worried. The office was a madhouse, with pet emergencies everywhere. No one could tell me where my little Jaké was. I finally screamed enough that someone paid attention to me. The news wasn't good.

Jaké was not used to strangers, so she squirmed excessively while they were trimming her nails and they accidentally cut her foot. Since she was bleeding, they put a cast on her leg, but the bleeding hadn't stopped. She also wouldn't calm down and until she did, they didn't want to bring her to me.

"Of course she won't calm down," I screamed. "She needs her Mommy."

I threatened the receptionist until a tech took me to her. The tech walked me through the squeaky swinging door to a very busy back room. The tech had placed Jaké's cage in an oxygen chamber on the bottom of a rack in the room where they weighed the really large dogs. She was petrified! I grabbed her cage and took her to an empty examination room where I could hold her. She was scared, but now that Mom was there, she was definitely better.

I packed her up to take her home. As we walked out, the receptionist said to me, "There will be no charge for today." I just glared at her.

You bet there will be no charge. And once this cast comes off, I won't be returning, either.

I spent most of the day holding Jaké, mostly because I was worried about her, but also because she couldn't do much with the cast on her leg. She could only stand on a flat surface. Climbing or sitting on her perch was out of the question, as was flying since the cast weighed nearly as much as she did, so I felt the most comforting thing I could do was to keep her close.

When it was time for her to go nite-nite, I put her on one of the pillows on my bed. I thought it would be softer for her, not thinking that birds don't like to be out in the open like that. I went back to check on her about a half hour later, and she had gimped her way to the foot of the bed! She wanted to be with me.

I put her back on the pillow and explained to her that it would be much more comfortable to be there and she needed her rest after such a traumatic day, but when I found her at the foot of the bed once again 15 minutes later, I scooped her up and kept her with me until *I* was ready for nite-nite.

I climbed into bed and put her on the pillow next to me, thinking she would stay there the whole night now that I was close by. I had had an exhausting day worrying about her, so I fell asleep quickly and didn't think about it again.

When I awoke the next morning, I was sleeping on my right side. I didn't know where Jaké was. I assumed she was on the other pillow where I had left her the night before. I reached back and patted the pillow with my left hand, but she wasn't there! Now I was frantic. Had she fallen on the floor? Had she moved to the foot of the bed? Was she under the covers? I didn't think that she could go very far without me, but she had an iron will so with her, anything was possible. I called to her, but she didn't answer. My stomach churned with fear. What if she didn't make it through the night?

I wanted to roll over onto my back so I could better assess the situation. Since I didn't know where she was, I first put my arm out behind me to feel for her on the bed in the area I couldn't see. I touched something soft and ...sleeping! My heart leapt with joy! Jaké, my baby, was sound asleep, cuddled against the small of my back. Never before had I ever experienced such a beautiful moment. She felt protected by me, and she had no fear to lean against me in the dark.

The cast came off later that afternoon and Jaké was back to her independent self. It was as if nothing had ever happened. From that day forward, I never let her alone at the vet again, except for one frightening episode I'll explain later. I immediately decided her life was worth more than a drive across town, and promptly switched vets. She still got scared when she heard the squeak of the swinging door while waiting in the office for her appointment. However, from that time on, we had two very caring vets who let me stay with her while she got her nails trimmed.

We did have one major episode during her egg laying years where I couldn't be with her in the examination room. She usually laid an egg every other day when she was brooding. This particular time, after she had laid two eggs, something changed. It was her day to lay. But, when I went to her cage, she just sat there, motionless, and totally nonresponsive. I was sick! She seemed perfectly fine when I went to bed, and now she seemed like a stuffed version of herself, so lifeless.

I immediately called the vet and rushed across town. He took one look at her and did an x-ray. The results: Jaké was egg-bound[2]. That meant that she had an egg that she couldn't dislodge for some reason. It could mean it wasn't fully formed and clung to some part of her anatomy. It might be too big for her to lay, or who knows what. The vet said he'd had success before with putting birds under anesthesia for just a few minutes. It relaxes the laying muscles and the egg just pops out.

I was game until he told me the bad news. She might not survive the anesthetic, or if the egg is attached to part of her insides, it could come out with the egg, and she could bleed to death. I was frantic, but there was nothing I could do. She needed to have the operation or she would die regardless. I had complete trust in the vet, as he had years of experience with birds. Still, there was a possibility this would be the last time I'd see her alive.

I held her for several minutes before he took her away. I heard the scary swinging doors, just like every veterinary hospital has, and off she went to her operation. The second hand on my watch refused to budge. Every beat felt like an hour. I called my sister and let her know what was happening. And I prayed.

In about 15 minutes, I heard the swinging doors again. The doctor came back and said everything was fine. The egg popped out just like he had hoped, and she was in recovery from the anesthetic. In about a half hour, I'd be able to take her home!

I was so thankful to have my baby back. We went home and immediately took a nice, long nap.

---

[2]Words from my vet: Pet birds such as cockatiels that lay eggs frequently or become "chronic egg-layers" can become egg-bound, which is a life-threatening condition and needs veterinary attention. Anytime a bird is unable to lay an egg on her own and she needs veterinary attention to help get the egg out, it is considered "egg-bound." Sometimes it is relatively easy and requires just fluids and warmth, sometimes anesthesia and massaging the egg out, and sometimes major surgery to get the egg out and spay the bird at the same time. This last procedure is risky for a bird. The smaller the bird, the riskier the procedure.

Chapter Twenty-One

Sharing my salad and hiding in the basket

Jaké always had a good appetite. She pretty much devoured her seed cakes once she got onto that eating plan, and she loved her big, blue pellets. However, she was also interested in eating my food.

Taco Bell was always something she was attracted to, probably because I ate it so often and she loved the smell of the hot sauce. However, I do eat other things, too. Salads are a particular favorite. As I made my salads, she'd either be in the bowl or the plate, nibbling on the lettuce or cucumbers. It didn't matter how many treats I'd already given her that day, for some reason, she found my salad to be more appealing.

I've rarely eaten a piece of lettuce that didn't have a beak bite in it. As for the cucumbers, if I didn't get them with seeds in them, she lectured me. Like I can control whether or not the cucumber has seeds! And, since when do cucumbers *not* have seeds? I like them too, Jaké.

In the heat of summer, Jaké loved to climb onto my plate of nice, cool vegetables, doing her little happy dance routine. I eventually realized that whenever she did that, she was ready for a bath. Since she now had the run of the house when I was home, I wasn't able to spray her as the vet instructed. I had to rely on clues from my little baby that she was ready for a bath.

I'd take my salad plate away and replace it with her blue dish full of water and she went to town. She'd splash and play and get herself all sopping wet! Then, she'd fly to the top of her cage and just sit there and shiver for a few minutes, before she preened. When she was done with that, it would be another few months before she was interested in getting wet again.

I've heard of people using a blow dryer to dry their birds after a bath, or holding them closely under a towel to keep them warm. I wasn't too keen on the blow dryer idea, and Jaké would never have allowed me to hold her with a towel, so she just shivered until she warmed up. The house was always warm, summer or winter, and luckily she never caught cold. I feel, for the most part, she knew what was best for her, so I just let her do her thing.

Aside from the veggies, like a mom, I worried about the other things she ate. Would they affect her in some way? Nacho chips always garnered her attention. Not only were her olfactory senses good, she had keen hearing as well. She could be in the bathroom sound asleep while I'd be in the kitchen opening a bag of chips. Before I could turn around to grab a drink, she was on my shoulder! If I put a chip in my mouth, she bit my mouth and licked up the crumbs. If I put her down on the counter and gave her a small piece of a chip, she devoured it in 10 seconds flat.

Every bite she took, I reprimanded myself for not following the rules I was given when she was just a little girl. I promised my first vet I'd take the very best care of her and I'm certain nacho chips were not on her list of "allowed" foods. But, you can't tell that to the *Divatiel*!

If Jaké saw me eating the chips – and mind you, I didn't buy them very often – she expected me to share with her immediately. At first, she yelled, either from the counter or from my shoulder directly into my ear. She knew how much I hated that! If I still didn't share, she flew onto my hand and bit my fingers, not the chip.

Then, in a flash, she was on my face, trying to lick up every savory morsel. When I shooed her off from there, she went onto my chest, hoping to catch a crumb or two. I realized the only way for me to snack in peace was to break off a small piece of chip and put it on the counter. This would take her a few seconds to find, then a few seconds to devour. By then, I could scarf down a few chips myself, close up the bag and put it back in the pantry.

"Chiiirrrppp!!! I want more chips! Feed me those wretched chips!!!"

"Jaké, all gone! Momma put them away. No more tonight. All gone."

I spread my hands open in front of her, like a mother often does to her young child, indicating that there was nothing left.

She'd eye my hands, one to the other, then look *me* in the eye. She really wanted more, but she seemed accepting whenever I hit her with the "all gone" move. She would give me the *'Chirp' of understanding*, climb onto my hand, and off we'd go to another adventure in *Divatieldom*.

In addition to eating, Jaké liked to tear things apart. Aside from the newspapers and greeting cards that she rendered useless all over the counter, Jaké also enjoyed baskets.

In some of the homes we lived, there was a display space between the top of the kitchen cupboards and the ceiling. So, I displayed stuff. In addition to some art, I placed flowers and a few vases, all of which Jaké ignored. She did occasionally play with the bell on Millennial Bear. But when it came to the baskets, well… let's just say it was amazing how quickly a four ounce bundle of joy could totally destroy an 18 inch wicker basket!

I had a red basket above the cabinets that totally excited Jaké. I suspect she was attracted to the color, but I can't imagine how much paint she imbibed. I'd always been good about keeping her away from the numerous other unhealthy items she attempted to devour, like grout, caulk and staples, but the basket way up high on the cabinet was out of reach, and Jaké knew it.

I think part of the rending process was hormonal, building a nest for her future fledglings. Part of it was just letting out frustration, part was just playing and part was building a safe hiding place. She ripped out a back section of the basket like a private passageway so she could enter and depart easily out of reach from that evil

Mommy. Or, if we had any visitors, the basket was like a castle turret, way up high. She felt safe there.

Occasionally, Jaké would throw a piece of basket over the top and just watch it fall. I'm not sure if she wanted to hit me with it or if she was just intrigued with the activity, almost like a science experiment.

Once Jaké discovered the basket, it became her daytime sanctuary. She'd nap in it, nest in it, lay her eggs in it and hide in it. If I went out for a few hours and I couldn't find her, eventually she'd climb to the top of the basket, spread her wings to say hello, give me a big chirp, and fly down to her cage where she'd eat or drink. Periodically, she'd hang out there even when I was home. Jaké was very independent and didn't always want to be with me. I'd sit for hours at the computer and some days, she refused to join me. So, she'd hang out in her basket.

When it came time to move to the next house, I climbed on a ladder to pick up her basket to pack it. It completely fell apart in my hands! She knew just what sections she could tear and still keep the basket together. I, on the other hand, didn't have the instinct that Jaké had; one touch and it all collapsed.

When we got to the new house, Mommy bought Jaké a new basket.

Living in the desert requires everyone to drink a lot of water. The air is very dry and it's important to keep hydrated. Birds don't drink very much, but it's important that they have access to water at all times.

When Jaké slept in her cage, her food and water were easy to reach. She could get up at any time of the night and take a sip. She wouldn't eat during the night, but on occasion, she'd climb down off her perch and drink.

Over time, Jaké was sleeping on the shower door. At first, she only slept there until I went to bed, then she went into her cage until morning. Eventually, she slept on the shower door all night. At some point, I realized that Jaké might get thirsty. After all, she was sleeping for upwards of 12 hours on many nights. So, I brought her water one time. And she took it!

From then on, I always brought water to her just before I went to sleep. Most nights, she didn't want anything and she let me know in her kindest hissing hysteria. I just had to walk into the bathroom and she knew what I was planning to do. I didn't even have to get near her before she started to inform me that she didn't want a drink. But some nights she took a gulp gladly and I was relieved that I took the time to quench her thirst. After all, it was my job as the Mommy/servant to anticipate the *Divatiel's* wishes and fulfill them!

Chapter Twenty-Two

Time to move – again!

"CHIIRRRPPP!!!"

"Yes, Jaké. We're moving again."

"Hiss."

I had to agree. Still, for a number of reasons, it was time to move. We were staying in Las Vegas, but a smaller house was definitely in order. The big house had the master bedroom and my office on the first floor, so I hardly ever went upstairs. During the summer months, the cost of cooling the second story was crazy expensive, considering it only was used when company came. And, most of the time, they stayed in a hotel, so their overnight visits to the house were few and far between.

I also realized that a southwest facing backyard was not the best in the desert heat. I dreamt of sipping wine while watching sunsets on the patio, but particularly during the summer months, it was so hot in the backyard, I didn't want to go out until about midnight.

I loved having all the space, but in actuality, it was costly to maintain and I really wasn't making the best use of it. After careful consideration, I decided the best thing to do was move.

"It's okay, Jaké. I promise to find a house where you can stay on top of the cabinets, and be able to see me from the shower door when you sleep. Momma will make sure it's the perfect house for us!"

I didn't believe it and neither did she, but the search was on for a new abode.

I loved the area where I was living, but I couldn't find anything I liked right away. I had considered moving back to California, but the thought of moving away from my family again was troubling. Still, I missed California terribly, and all my clients were there. So, until I decided where I was going to live for the next several years, rather than purchase, I rented.

We moved to a house less than half the size of our mini-mansion and stayed there for a year. Eventually, we found a place a little farther north of where we were living but closer to family. It was even smaller which meant I had to part with a lot of stuff, but it felt like home. In fact, it became home for many years.

Much Smaller House

Chapter Twenty-Three

New adventures atop the cabinets

Our new abode was a mere 1360 square feet with a very open floor plan. So, once again – new house, new habits to learn.

I took great care to select the front bedroom as my office so Jaké could have nearly a straight shot down the hallway and onto my shoulder.

The master bedroom had a double door entry so she could easily cut the corner flying from the kitchen onto the shower door. It often became a place of refuge. Whenever she was scared, she'd fly into the bathroom to hide. She was perfectly capable of making the return flight, but unless she heard me opening a bag of chips, she only made the ride on the Mommy limo and screeched until I picked her up!

Another favorite hangout was above the kitchen cabinets. There was a great open space, and I chose not to decorate them as much as I had in the past. I put a new basket on top for her lair, but the house came with a silk plant in the corner and Jaké soon discovered this was a great place to hide, nap and espy from a place of safety. As usual, it took her no time to rehab and decorate it to her taste. I just had to look out for falling debris!

Once I opened Jaké's cage door and introduced her to our new house, she quickly flew to the cabinet tops. I kept unpacking and I could hear her little feet tracking back and forth across the cabinets. Then, I didn't hear anything. I thought, *Oh, no, another cabinet accident!* I had already covered all the holes on top and I didn't hear her fall, but I couldn't find her anywhere!

I went to every room in the house, looked in every corner, checked every open box and Jaké was nowhere to be found! I didn't hear her fly, so I thought she might still be in the kitchen, but my baby had disappeared into thin air.

All of a sudden, something caught my eye. Up in the corner, behind the silk plant, I thought I saw some movement.

"Jaké! Jaké, is that you? Come out of there!"

Sure enough it was her. I could hear her squeak, that little noise she made whenever she was annoyed with me.

"Jaké! What are you doing up there? Come out where I can see you. I want to make sure you're okay."

As a *Divatiel* does, she ignored the commands of her owner. I banged on the cupboard directly below her hideout.

"Hiss!" Crunch, crunch.

"Jaké, don't be eating that basket! You can eat the one Momma bought for you over in the other corner. That one has to stay pretty."

All quiet.

I banged on the cabinet again.

Rustle, rustle. Out came the princess. With attitude. Just to hiss at me.

After her little show of annoyance, she took a look around and quickly shuffled backwards until she was well hidden behind the plant. Aside from that first time, she never ate that particular basket again even though she nearly demolished the other one. But, she did hang out in the corner almost every day.

These new cabinets had plenty of room to play up on top, but they didn't have the trim molding that the previous houses did. So, when Jaké hung out on the edge of the cabinets, she literally was on the edge! Her little toes would hang over so casually while she watched me from up above.

The edge of the cabinets was generally not an issue unless I needed to get into one of them.

"Watch your feet! Jaké, watch your feet!" I'd tell her as I opened a cabinet door.

Slowly, Jaké would shuffle back just enough for me to get the door open and remove what I needed. Once I closed the door, she was back on the edge again. I had to remind her to "Watch your feet!" again, so her toes wouldn't get caught as the cupboard door closed.

Occasionally, Jaké preferred to go along for the ride. Instead of backing up while I opened the door, she instead jumped onto it and swung back and forth while I gathered what I wanted. *Back and forth, back and forth.* She'd race across the top of the cabinets trying to figure out which one I would open next so she could go there and ride the door.

Snoopy was also interested in what was inside the cabinets so, sometimes once the door was open, she hung upside down checking it out. She didn't want to miss a possible hideout, and dark spaces always intrigued her. I had to warn her to back up again so I could close the door, which of course was followed by a hiss, and sometimes she'd fly to my shoulder to yell at me, then fly back on top.

"Momma loves you too, baby."

Chapter Twenty-Four

Behaving for the babysitter

"Jaké, Mommy is going out of town for a few days."

"Chirp."

"Seriously, are you paying attention to me? Or are you just enjoying me scratching your head?"

"Chirp."

Sometimes, I got the *'Chirp' of understanding*. Other times, I got a patronizing chirp. I was never quite sure which was which.

I know my little *Divatiel* was truly intelligent, but this particular experience really showed me just how smart she was.

As I've said before, Jaké slept on the shower door in my bathroom, and she clearly knew how to fly from there to the kitchen where her food, drink and treats were. However, she refused to do it. When she was ready to get up, she started with chirps that only increased in intensity if she was particularly hungry and I was nonresponsive. It was my job to pick her up and carry her to the kitchen.

Now, one benefit of me carrying her was the constant kisses. From the time she climbed onto my hand until we were in the kitchen, I kissed her. Constantly. Probably 20 kisses in those few steps. Definitely something I looked forward to. I'm not so sure about her.

Usually when I traveled, I'd take her to my sister's house. However, this time was different. The entire family was heading out of town to throw a surprise birthday party for my Mom. I could have found someone to take care of her, or board her at the vet, but she would have had to stay in her cage the entire time in a strange place.

Jaké was getting older, and I worried more and more how changes would affect her. By now, she was already 18 years old, at the top of the average age for household cockatiels. I thought long and hard about what to do with her in my absence. I decided to swallow the cost and made a phone call.

I hired a pet sitter so Jaké could stay in the house where she was most comfortable. The sitter would come around 10 in the morning to feed her, open the shutters and turn on the television. Around 7 p.m. or so she'd return so Jaké could eat her dinner and go nite-nite.

As Jaké was such a spoiled *Divatiel*, I was really worried that she would never leave the bathroom and would starve to death before I returned from my week's vacation. A few days before I left, I began telling her what I wanted her to do.

> *Now, Jaké, I know that you know how to fly from the bathroom to the kitchen all by yourself, and then back to the bathroom to go nite-nite. And I know that you won't let the sitter come near you because you don't know her. So, you're going to have to be a big girl while Momma's out of town. When the sitter comes in the morning, you'll have to fly to the kitchen all by yourself so you can eat and drink. Then, you can stay there or in the living room all day. When she comes back at night, you need to eat your dinner, then fly by yourself to the bathroom so you can go nite-nite. You need to do this every day, okay?*

Every time I scratched Jaké's head for those few days, I would repeat the same thing. Jaké gave me her *'Chirp' of understanding*, and just twisted and turned her head to make sure I got all the little feathers. I knew she was listening, I knew she was smart but I wasn't quite sure how she would behave while I was out of town. I knew I'd be a nervous wreck for seven days.

I set up an agreement with the sitter that she would only call me in an emergency. Otherwise, I knew there was nothing I could do 2,000 miles away from her. I left instructions for my vet so the sitter could go there in an emergency. I trusted the sitter fully so, although I was worried, I just had to focus on being with my family and enjoying myself. Jaké and I hadn't been separated that long for awhile, but I just had to trust everything would be all right.

I gave good-bye kisses to Jaké, left a check for the sitter, and headed for the airport.

About three days into my trip, my cell phone rang. It was the sitter. I was shaking, my heart was racing. I nearly dropped the phone.

"What's wrong? What's wrong with Jaké?"

I was beside myself with worry, and my heart was pumping a mile a minute. After all, she was an older bird, and birds in general are so very fragile. I just couldn't bear the thought of her not being there when I got back.

"Nothing. She's perfectly fine," the sitter said, much to my relief. "She was just playing and chirping, so I thought you might want to hear her voice. I'll put you on speaker so you can talk to her, too."

I listened to Jaké, and it was music to my ears. And, I guess Jaké stopped what she was doing, turned her head and listened to me.

"You know, there is something else I wanted to talk to you about."

Oh, no, here it comes. I knew it couldn't be all good news.

"It's the funniest thing. When I open the door in the morning and call to Jaké, she immediately flies from the bathroom into the kitchen. Then, after she eats at night, she flies back into the bathroom. It's like clockwork every day. Wow! You really have her trained!"

Jaké had never done that in her life. I was thrilled that my little girl was behaving just as I asked her. What a proud mother I was!

When I got back from my trip, it was about 11 p.m. Jaké was already nite-nite and she was actually astonished to hear my voice and see me back in my bedroom. When I woke the next morning, I figured she had spent a week behaving like a big girl, so I was excited to see her fly to the kitchen when she wanted to get up.

I was drinking my tea and reading the paper when I heard that familiar "come and get me" chirp. I reminded her that she had been a big girl all week, and I was waiting in the kitchen whenever she was ready. No matter how I reasoned with her, the chirps just became louder and more demanding.

I finally went into the bathroom, whereupon she stopped yelling, bowed down and spread her wings for me, then waited until I put my hand out for her so I could carry and kiss her into the kitchen.

Yep, who's the master here?

Chapter Twenty-Five

Separation anxiety

Shortly after my vacation to celebrate my Mom's birthday, I made two more back-to-back trips. For these, we went through the usual routine of Jaké going to my sister's house and staying in her cage. Jaké was never thrilled about this, but I knew she would have someone with her pretty much 24/7 and that was important to me. It was also very expensive to have a competent sitter come to the house twice a day. So, I had to weigh Jaké's preference versus her safety and cost.

Once I returned from my second trip, I could tell something was different about Jaké. Although she was thrilled to have me home, she had suddenly developed some sort of separation anxiety. She was constantly fearful that I was going to leave her again, and for a few weeks, she became exceptionally clingy. I couldn't move more than a foot or two away from her before she either yelled or flew to me. Although we'd been together for a long time, this was the first time she showed such emotions.

Our typical nite-nite routine was most affected. Generally, Jaké screeched a certain screech when it was time to go nite-nite. I then took her into the bathroom where I wished her a good night's sleep, she bowed, and I turned off the light and left the room. She then selected which end of the shower was more comfortable, depending on the season, and went to sleep peacefully, waiting patiently for me to go nite-nite as well.

If I didn't get her into the bathroom quickly enough from the time she let out her first nite-nite screech, she flew there on her own. Then, the next screech came, informing me I had to turn off the light. As a habit, once dusk came, I turned on the bathroom light because she also flew there if she got scared and she couldn't see in the dark. So, once she was there for nite-nite, I had to hustle to turn off the light. If, for some reason I couldn't get to it immediately, she'd screech for a few minutes, then finally give up and go to sleep. And, when I did make it to darken her sleep area, she hissed at me.

If all was normal and I reacted within my 60 second window, she would cuddle up against the tile on the shower wall. I wished her a good night's sleep, told her I'd be going to bed shortly, and made my way back out of the bedroom. The second she couldn't see me, she called to me. I had to walk back toward her and truly convince her that it was OK for her to go to sleep without me. This routine got shorter, but it used to last 30 minutes. Remember, this is a bird that had been spoiled by me for over 14 years, and she still didn't trust that I'd be there for her!

Once I convinced her that everything was OK, I was free to move about my house as I pleased. Unless she decided to test me. Maybe 15 minutes or so after Jaké had gone nite-nite, she'd let out a 'bloody-murder, I need you right now' screech. I'd go rushing into the bathroom to make sure she was OK, and she was. She was just checking to see that I hadn't left the house.

Often, she'd be on the front part of the shower door and as soon as she saw me, she bent down to spread her wings to tell me she loved me. Then she'd go to sleep. She had to bow and show me her wings every single night or she couldn't go to sleep. She usually bowed from atop her cage. If she forgot, I'd get that insistent call from her in the shower, and she'd spread her wings there.

After my travels, she really didn't trust that I was going to go nite-nite shortly as I promised, particularly since she knew I was a night owl. So, for weeks, and I do mean weeks, I had to go to bed when she did. She screamed so loudly and so hurtfully that I was afraid she would injure herself if she kept it up for too long. I tried to keep her up but the princess was tired and wanted to go to sleep. Mommy liked to stay up late. Luckily, Jaké was going to sleep later in the evening and, although I wasn't happy about going to sleep at 10 o'clock, eventually Jaké learned that I was sticking around and she went back to her former nite-nite routine.

Chapter Twenty-Six

Facing fears

Routine. Routine. Routine. Jaké totally loved routine. From the time we got up in the morning till the time we went to bed, she did pretty much the same thing. And, she expected me to do the same. Spontaneity was not in her vocabulary.

Our pre-nite-nite routine was very much the same every day. It was important to her that she bowed and showed her wings to me, usually from the edge of her cage. She just couldn't bear to go to sleep without bowing. When she bowed, I always told her how beautiful she was, and I finished with, "Thank you for bowing, baby."

But, it got to the point where she watched me as she did it, to make sure I was looking at her and not just commenting to the air. She was very adamant that I watched her while she bowed and spoke directly to her. If she bowed and I didn't notice for some reason, she banged her wing against the cage until I looked directly at her and told her how beautiful she was. She watched me the entire time to make sure I wasn't just saying it but I really meant it. She had me trained!

When it was time for Momma to go nite-nite, I took water to her in the bathroom to see if she was thirsty. She'd either take a drink or hiss the minute she saw me coming. However, it was also a hint to her that I was starting my bedtime routine.

After I returned the water to her cage in the kitchen and turned off all the lights, I walked back into the bathroom and spoke to her at the shower. She'd sit on the edge of the shower door, waiting for a digest of what was to come tomorrow. She waited patiently for me, head cocked to one side; with bated breath she clung to my every word.

> *Pumpkin, Momma go sleep, you go sleep, too, okay? Good night. Momma loves you, baby, nite-nite. If you need Momma, you call me, okay? Momma loves you, baby, nite-nite.*

That was all fine and dandy, but that wasn't the most interesting part as far as Jaké was concerned. What followed was critical to how *her* next day would be. There were three options. The first:

> *Momma has to get up early tomorrow morning. It will be dark outside when Momma gets up because I have a meeting tomorrow and I have to get up.*

This was usually followed by a nasty hiss. The second option:

> *Momma has to get up early tomorrow but you get to sleep in, okay?*

This was acceptable behavior from Jaké's perspective, but not her favorite. At least it meant that I would be home. The third option:

> *Guess what, pumpkin? We get to sleep in tomorrow! Yes, we get to sleep in!*

Obviously, this was Jaké's favorite. No alarm clock. The sun was up when we got up. And best of all, Momma would be in bed where she could see me. When she'd hear me say those magic words, you could see the happiness in her face. She'd stretch her wings and sidle over to her corner, cuddle up and go to sleep. It was the most amazing thing.

Mornings were always tough. No sunshine allowed peeking through the windows too early. Shutters were closed tight, and I even bought curtains to cover the glass block windows in the bathroom to keep out those morning rays. It was dark as dark could be – with a night light, of course – until *we* determined it was time to get up.

Since Jaké and I both liked to sleep in, those days that I had to be on the road at some very early hour were rough on both of us.

Before I went to sleep, I always had my little conversation with Jaké. If I told Jaké we'd get to sleep in, she didn't care what else I had to say before I turned off the lights. She shook her feathers and went to sleep. If I told her we had to get up early, she just stared at me, as if she were thinking, "You've got to be kidding! Don't you know I like to sleep in?" Well, baby, I like to sleep in, too, but sometimes, duty calls.

When I got up in the morning, regardless of the time, I always let her get a few extra winks. I'd wash my hands and dry them on a towel near the shower door, at which point she turned into *spawn of Satan*, hissing and screaming at me for disturbing her slumber. Then she cuddled back up until I returned to fetch her for breakfast.

On those difficult mornings where I was out the door by 7 a.m., it was a whole different story. I let Jaké sleep until the last possible minute. When I was ready to leave, I'd head to the bathroom to pick her up and bring her into the kitchen. And, let me tell you, it was a rough way to start the day.

Once at the shower door I'd tell Jaké it was time for Momma to leave. She'd just sit there, giving me the *Evil Eye*. I couldn't possibly be interfering with the princess's beauty sleep, now could I? Alas, I was.

When she didn't move toward me, which was most mornings, I had to climb into the shower to reach her. I'd put my hand flat against her little tummy and, ever so slowly, she plopped one foot, then the other, on my hand. Once there, she screamed and nibbled my fingers in protest.

We'd make our way into the kitchen where she took no more than three seconds to fly up on top of the cupboards, scurry herself backwards and take a nap behind the silk plant in the corner.

I suspect she slept for awhile, although I really don't know since I wasn't at home those days. It was dark behind the plant, affording her the opportunity to get a bit more shuteye before she winged it down to the table to have some breakfast.

On those mornings when she was really mad about getting up, she did the unthinkable – she flew to the ledge connecting my bedroom and bathroom, a place where she knew I couldn't reach her without a step ladder. One time she walked side to side, knocking down clumps of dust in protest. I may not always have had a step ladder at the ready, but I learned she hated to see a yard stick. Once that came out, she made her way down in a huff. I felt badly those mornings because I like to ease myself into the day and that sort of activity stressed us both out.

If I only planned to be away a few hours, I promised we'd take a nap when I returned, and that seemed to make her happy. Naptime was second only to nite-nite as Jaké's favorite activity, so I usually was forgiven for awakening her so early.

If I'd been gone all day and we were up really early, Jaké was ready for nite-nite early, too. So, I'd come home, have a bite to eat, as would she, and then the screeching would start. Not only was Jaké ready for nite-nite, she expected me to join her, just like she required after my recent travels. Most times I could convince her that I had some very important work to do before I went to sleep, but she didn't always believe me. She'd scream and scream from the shower until I turned off all the lights and went to bed. Ah, isn't bonding fun!

Once the lights were off and we were sound asleep, Jaké was usually quiet. I assumed she didn't move a stitch for the entire night. The room was dark, but Jaké needed her night light on for comfort, and to see where she was should she have to fly off in the dark. There was a small light above the sinks, kind of like a crescent moon in her night sky.

On occasion, birds do have night frights. I guess they're equivalent to nightmares in humans, but I can't be sure. When Jaké slept in her cage, she did occasionally have a night fright, which scared the heck out of me! But, once she started sleeping on top of the shower door, things were a little different.

In Jaké's case, I'm not so certain she had night frights per se. I had seen her where she was so sound asleep, she appeared to just roll off her perch, causing her to lose her balance and be frightened. In the case of the shower door, I think she moved from side to side during the night and occasionally lost her footing, winding up in the bottom of the shower or bathtub.

One night I was awakened at about 3 a.m. Jaké had screamed and I heard some wings fluttering, then a *Whoomp*! I wasn't sure what happened, but like a Mom with a newborn baby, I was up in a flash. I found Jaké sitting in the sink! She looked petrified, as I'm sure anyone would be who flew around in the night and wound up in a sink.

I picked her up and held her close to calm her down. I usually turned on the lights when this happened but for some reason, I didn't do it that moment. I held her close for awhile, but my alarm was going off in a couple of hours and I needed to get back to bed.

I put her on top of the shower door, but instead of cuddling up, she spread her wings and kept looking down to the bottom of the shower. I had no idea what she was looking at. Smartly, instead of chalking it up to *Divatiel* idiosyncrasies, I turned on the light. There in the bottom of the shower stall was a big, brown bug!

No wonder Jaké was scared. I was, too! I swooped in with wads of tissue, wished the bug a good next life, and smashed it to smithereens. To Jaké, I was her hero. She bowed for me, then walked to the corner, leaned her head against the tile, and fell quickly asleep.

Jaké hated to see the darkness outside. I always tried to be home before it got dark. It scared her for some reason. Maybe because she couldn't see what was happening in the dark. If I knew I'd be home after the sun went down, I'd leave lights on for her. Still, she preferred me to close the blinds, too. However, if I was going to be gone for several hours, I liked her to enjoy the daylight as much as she could.

My vets had always told me birds that are flighted can get into trouble if you're not home, so it's important to keep the bird in the cage when you're away. Jaké was never thrilled about being in the cage once she learned to fly, but I kept up the routine, even in our new house. As long as I was home, she had all the freedom in the world, but when I left, she went inside. Even in the cage with the lights on, when it got dark outside, Jaké was unhappy and fearful.

One day, I was running late from an appointment. It was getting dark, but I had one more stop to make before I went home. I didn't leave a light on for Jaké, but she was in her cage, so I figured she'd be safe. There were nightlights on in the house.

That should be enough light for her, I thought. *I'll be home only about 20 minutes after sundown.*

I felt confident that she was fine, so I completed my errand. I could have done it the next day, but I wanted to stay home and have just one day that week I didn't have to leave the house. So, imagine the guilt I felt when I walked in the door and turned on the lights.

Jaké was huddled in the bottom of her cage, blood and feathers everywhere. I didn't even know if she was alive. No errand was worth the life of my baby. None. Ever.

She finally turned her head, so I knew there was hope. I knew how she was when it got dark outside, and I could say with confidence that was not what caused her condition. However, I had no idea what did.

Something obviously had frightened her. And, because she was locked in the cage, she couldn't escape. She was stuck. I made a decision right then and there that when – not if – she got better, I'd allow her to stay out of the cage when I wasn't home.

A lot of people will say that's not a good idea. But I knew my baby, and she was generally a good girl. She wasn't a dog or a cat that dumped over the trash or tore apart pillows when the master was out. She tended to hang out in the same places in the house and I felt I could trust her. From that day on, she rarely went into a locked cage. She had the run of the house, so if something scared her, she could fly or she could hide, but she didn't have to feel trapped.

Jaké slept for three or four days, nonstop, trying to recover. She couldn't fly. She had lost so many feathers, it was worse than a molt. I had to carry her everywhere. She was devastated. You could see the disappointment in her eyes. She had a broken spirit. Jaké was a very independent *Divatiel*, and her inability to do what she wanted was heartbreaking.

She'd try to fly, but until her feathers grew back in, she couldn't get farther than a few feet. She'd give it all she had, and I was worried she'd hurt herself even more because she didn't have that *oomph* that she needed to provide distance and lift. I felt her pain.

Jaké continued her recovery, trying to fly, pushing herself harder and harder everyday with the same disappointing outcome. She'd just look at me with those "Help, Mom!" eyes, and there was nothing I could do about it. I kept telling her it would take about six weeks for her feathers to grow back in, but that didn't dissuade her from giving it her all every single time. I wish I had that gusto.

Then, one day, she was really tired of me babying her. She liked to be cared for, but she also liked to be in charge. She didn't want to totally depend upon me. I carried her into the kitchen and, like the little engine that could, she willed herself to fly to the top of the cabinets.

She made it! Once on top, her demeanor changed completely. She let out a loud chirp as if to say, "Yeah, I'm back!" ruffled her feathers and pranced delightedly across the top of the cabinets. My baby was happy once again!

There was still the issue of what did scare her. I was stumped. Anything can scare a bird, but for her to react so intensely, it had to be something unusual.

A few weeks later, I was washing dishes in the kitchen sink. Something big and white in the sky caught my eye. I thought maybe it was sunlight reflecting off an airplane, because it was big and quick. I didn't think too much about it.

A couple of hours later, Jaké was sitting on top of her cage, preening calmly, looking out the patio door into the backyard. In a split second, she screeched the loudest screech I had ever heard, flew straight up, then frantically into the living room, hit the wall and fell into a bucket! An empty bucket, thank goodness.

I looked out the window and at first, I didn't see anything. Then, there it was. The snowy white object I had seen in the sky was back. In my yard! It was a four foot tall egret, prancing around as if it owned the place. They may look beautiful from afar, but when one is within a couple of feet of you, you realize the power in those birds and I definitely didn't want a face to face encounter.

It traversed my yard and headed straight to my pond. One by one, it had a little snack - my goldfish. Then I remembered how that day began.

I went out to feed my fishies, and on a rock surrounding the pond, there was an eight inch long fish. I knew it wasn't one of my fish that jumped the pond. They were beautiful and colorful and definitely smaller. This was a big silvery grey fish. Did it just fall from the sky? I got some newspaper, wrapped it up and put it in the trash.

I now realized the fish came from this snowy white creature who obviously dropped it mid-flight. But, where in Las Vegas would you find an egret, let alone an egret with a fish?

Turns out, there's a housing subdivision about a half mile from my house that is built around a man-made lake. The lake is stocked with fish for the residents, and a few egrets and blue herons call this place home. I suspect this beautiful creature came for a visit the day Jaké injured herself, just based on the reaction Jaké had when she saw it moments before. Who could blame her?

Once the egret had enough hors d'oeuvres, it hopped across my yard and on top of the five foot tall fence in one big leap. Whew! Strong legs! Then, in another thrust, it was off into the sky and back to the lake.

When the ordeal was over, I rescued Jaké from the bucket. I now knew what had caused her such great fear, and I was grateful I was home to witness it for myself. It also reinforced my decision to let her be free when I was out of the house. Now, at least, she had options.

I never saw the egret again in the yard, but a blue heron did come to visit, not to snack. It brought its own fish and just sat and ate it. There's just something about my yard…

Chapter Twenty-Seven

More injuries for my baby

After the egret episode, Jaké always had the run of the house, whether or not I was home. For the most part, she hung out behind the silk plant in the corner of the cupboards, or in her basket. I always kept her cage in its normal location on the dining table with the door open and her food and water on the table with her treats spread out across the top of the cage. If I was out for several hours, she'd come down to eat and drink, then fly back to her hangout. And, if I was out at night, she'd often put herself nite-nite before I get home. What a good girl!

I have to admit, for the most part, Jaké was in good health. However, I didn't always know why Jaké might not act herself, or if she was injured for that matter. One night, I came home to find her huddled behind her cage. She occasionally did that, so I wasn't too worried until I looked a bit closer. She was shaking! She looked at me with such sad eyes; I just scooped her up and cuddled her.

After she calmed down, I thought maybe she wanted to eat, so I put her back down on her table near her food. At first, she just stood there. When she finally did move, she was limping, pretty badly. *Now* what happened?

I picked her up and looked her over, but she didn't appear to have any external injuries. Whatever happened obviously hurt, so I carried her around wherever I went. I tried to feed her, but she just turned her beak up at me, and closed her eyes for a nap. Now I was really worried. Jaké never refused to eat!

The next day, I took her to the vet. She checked her over and, from the outside, she appeared to be OK.

"We could do more tests, but because of her age, the tests could do her more harm than good and chances are they could be inconclusive," she said. "It's also possible she's developed arthritis. She is getting older, and these sorts of things may just happen."

I was stunned. Arthritis? All of a sudden? I couldn't believe that. Not possible. She seemed so young even though she was already 19 years old. But, to do more tests, other than a thorough blood test, the vet required her to go under anesthesia. Given her age, my vet was reluctant to proceed. Sure, she could pull through just fine, but there was a slight chance…

I didn't want to think about it, but I also didn't want to think about Jaké living a more restricted life. I guess none of us like to think along those terms even for ourselves. She was always so lively that for her to be confined would be heart wrenching, not only for me, but I wasn't sure how she would take it.

I packed Jaké up and took her back home. Since she wasn't eating, the vet gave me some baby bird food and a syringe. She said to try feeding her that periodically if she didn't eat for another day. She needed her strength as well as liquids to prevent dehydration.

If you think giving her a drop of calcium was difficult, try shoving food down her throat. She spit food everywhere! She hated it. I got a little bit in her beak, but after the second attempt, she decided it was better for her to eat her regular food than be subjected to me and the syringe. I didn't care how she got food inside of her, as long as she was eating.

Her appetite increased but aside from that, for several weeks, there was no physical improvement whatsoever. I called the vet again, and she said that if she had torn a ligament, chances are she'd never recover. Then she brought up the arthritis thing again.

At the time, I was writing an article about pet gifts, and one of the folks I interviewed was Tim Link, an animal communicator in Georgia. I know there are things that we just don't understand in this world, and I thought perhaps he could talk to her and at least find out what happened. Then, maybe we could set a course of correction.

I made the telephone appointment with Tim a couple of days later. The night before the call, Jaké was on her bookshelf in my office. The way she was acting caught my eye. She was turning her head side to side, up and down, and doing something akin to murmuring. I'd never seen her act like that before. After a few minutes, it stopped, and she curled up and took a nap.

The next day when Tim called, I told him how she had been the night before. He said that he was chatting with her, to get prepared for today's call. OK, so that explained it.

We got into the call, and Tim told me things about Jaké that I had never told him, nor had I expected to hear. But, the one thing he did tell me was what was wrong with her.

When a pet is injured, and Tim is communicating with the pet, his body hurts right where the pet's body hurts. In this case, it was his left leg. I hadn't told him that; I just mentioned that she was injured and I wanted to know what happened.

He said that she was showing him a picture of a basket up high, and that her leg got caught and she fell. Sure enough, Jaké had her basket on top of the cabinets that she climbed in and out of, and she hadn't gone near it since she hurt herself.

Tim wasn't sure how badly she was injured, or if she would recover, but he knew that it wasn't arthritis. He said to give it some time and see if she improves.

I was relieved to know what happened, but I was still dismayed that she wasn't getting any better. Jaké loved to be independent, and with her injury, she was very dependent upon me.

I thanked Tim for all his help, and got into my routine for the day; in fact, for a couple of days. On the third day, I noticed something different about Jaké. She was acting perfectly normal! No limping, lots of flying, climbing and sassing. Her normal self!

I was in shock. What could have brought about the change? I contacted Tim immediately, and he said that he sent some healing love Jaké's way, and thankfully, it worked. I was so grateful. There were no words to describe my appreciation.

I took Jaké to my vet to show her the difference. She was both impressed and curious. She said she'd heard about animal communicators before, but she hadn't personally experienced any of their work.

Once again, I packed Jaké up and took her home. She immediately shot out of the opened cage door and flew to the top of the cabinets. My baby was back once again.

Jaké flew around the house, wherever she darn well pleased. She also tended to fly into the bathroom onto the shower door when she was either scared or mad at me. She could be scared simply because I was cleaning and she thought that meant we were moving. We'd moved so many times, she got really scared every time she saw a box. I tried to explain to her what was going on, but it didn't always help.

One particular Sunday afternoon, she was flying back and forth from the kitchen to the bathroom. She was also giving me a special chirp that usually meant, *I have something to tell you and you need to guess what it is.* It was a similar chirp to when someone came to visit while I was out and I forgot to tell her we were going to have company.

I knew the neighbors weren't outside walking around, and the gardener didn't come on Sundays, so I was a bit perplexed as to what she needed to tell me. She looked at me very earnestly, like I should be able to read her mind. We were very close, so you'd think I could, but sometimes, I was just stumped.

About three hours or so after she started her little *chirpisode*, I happened to walk into the bathroom. There was blood everywhere! It seems she must have flown directly into the sharp corner of the shower stall and broke a blood feather. There was a long streak of blood down the glass, and drops on the towel and bathmat.

I ran into the kitchen and grabbed her to make sure she wasn't still bleeding. I took her into the bathroom and pointed out the blood.

"Is this what you were trying to tell me?" I asked.

She gave me the *'Chirp' of understanding.*

"I'm so sorry. I didn't know. Are you OK?"

She chirped again.

Once I recognized what she was yelling about, she quit yelling. Thankfully, she was fine but it scared the heck out of me. The bathroom looked like something out of a horror flick, yet she was completely clean and unbloodied. However, she knew that something was wrong and she persisted to make me understand.

Once I recognized what she was yelling about, she quit yelling. [illegible]

Chapter Twenty-Eight

Eating and sleeping

I once heard that cockatiels were the catfish of the bird world. Simply put, that means that they'll eat anything they encounter. Well, maybe not eat it, but definitely try it. They're like two-year-old children who put everything in their mouths. For example, Jaké was attracted to the dirt in the drain pan from the palm tree.

I believe catfish are bottom feeders, so for a bird, that means walking on the floor. I could always tell when it was time to mop or vacuum when Jaké spent more time than usual on the floor, and I could hear her crunching crumbs from one end of the kitchen to the other.

However, it wasn't my entire fault. Jaké had a hand in this, too. I'm sure she got tired of the same old routine, flying to the dining table – the entire dining table was hers, mind you – and eating from her dish.

So, when she was in the mood for a bit of a change, she simply flung the seed cakes, one by one, over the side of the table, and dropped to the floor to eat her dinner. She'd done this for years, ever since I introduced her to seed cakes. If I tried to pick her up and put her back on the table, she threw even more over the edge in defiance. So, I just let her be.

When she was done eating, she didn't fly back onto the table. Rather, she walked around the kitchen until she found me, stopped and looked up at me like a princess to her servant. I had to bend down to pick her up and put her where she wanted to go. I knew this because once I picked her up, she leaned her entire body in the preferred direction. When I finally reached her desired destination, she'd take a mini-flight and ignore me once again.

This wasn't a habit just for the floor feeding episodes. She did this all the time. If you watch birds in the wild, you'll see that they do a fair amount of walking on the ground, and Jaké was no different. She followed me around the house sometimes almost like a dog. If I walked slowly enough, she kept up. Sometimes, she'd chirp a conversation to me along the way. Almost like a pleasant after dinner stroll.

When she got to the point where she'd had enough, she simply stopped, looked up and waited for me to pick her up. If she had been a child, she'd have raised her arms yelling, "Mommy, up!"

I obligingly bent down and picked her up, usually planting her on my shoulder where she continued to accompany me on my treks through the house, keeping me company until she determined she was ready to do something else. It was like short attention span theater!

Jaké and I had very similar habits. I don't know if it was always that way, or if we just developed similarities as the years went by, like an old married couple who start to look like each other and finish each other's sentences.

We definitely both liked to sleep, and sleeping in was the best way to start the day. Once we were actually up, neither one of us liked to eat breakfast right away. I usually made my tea, read my emails and checked out the newspaper. After an hour or so, I started to think about what I might have for breakfast.

Jaké wasn't a morning person either. Once I eventually did get her up – she almost always slept longer than I did – I'd take her into the kitchen. There, she usually flew to the top of the refrigerator just to wake up and accustom herself to the day light. Then, she'd preen for a little bit, and sometimes even take a short nap. After about an hour, she'd fly to the kitchen table, take a drink of water, and contemplate eating. Then, she finally did.

If I knew I was going to be gone all day, I'd try to get her up a bit earlier than I normally would, and explain to her how long I'd be out. Then, I repeatedly told her she had to eat. Otherwise, she'd go all day without eating or drinking, even though it was right in front of her. If I could, I tried to get her to eat before I left, just for my own peace of mind.

Slowly but surely, Jaké made me her flock. Because of that, she hated for me to eat alone. Or, maybe *she* hated to eat alone. Jaké, unless she was absolutely famished, would wait for me to stand at the kitchen island for a period of time, so that I was there while she ate. Sometimes I was eating, too, but oftentimes, I just worked the crossword puzzle and kept her company.

Then that trust thing came into play. If I so much as budged from my spot, she noticed, squealed, and stopped eating. If I went farther than the refrigerator, she completely stopped and went behind her cage to observe what I was doing. If I walked into the living room to change the channel on the television, she thought I was leaving her and retreated to her faithful aerie behind the silk plant.

When I did get back to the kitchen island, which may have been a mere 30 seconds, it could take me 10-20 minutes to convince her that I wasn't going anywhere and I wanted her to eat. That's a lot of crossword puzzles! It was like I had a ball and chain attached to the island. I couldn't move an inch without her noticing.

I knew she needed to eat because I knew her stomach timetable, but she would get in her moods and suddenly she had to start this whole trust thing again. If she didn't eat on schedule, she got really crabby and bit and hissed.

Once she did start eating again, it could take her as long as 30 minutes to finish, which delayed my departure on more than one occasion. I waited because I knew she was hungry, and if she didn't eat at that time, it might be hours before I returned and she'd eat again.

On occasion, I came home and found that she had eaten in my absence. I always praised her, hoping she'd do it all the time, but she seemed amazed that I noticed and pledged to herself that she wouldn't do *that* again. So, she waited.

She also started a new routine for dinner time. Although she was perfectly capable of climbing up and down her cage to get to her food and her treats, when it came to dinner time, she chose only to climb up – then scream. Jaké's typical routine was to eat her seed cakes on the table, climb up her cage to get to her treats, then climb back down for another course.

Well, she was perfectly content to do that for breakfast and lunch, but come dinner time, things changed. She ate, drank, climbed, nibbled and screamed. She refused to slide back down for another round of seed cakes. Her scream was an indication that it was time for me to come over, put my hand out for her to climb onto, and place her gingerly back on the table in front of her food dishes.

She'd eat another round, climb back up, nibble on the lettuce and cucumbers, and scream! We'd go three or four rounds, until, instead of pointing her head downward when she was on my hand, she'd look me in the eye. That was the signal that it was nite-nite time.

As she got older, Jaké was more likely to wait for me to eat than when she was younger. I didn't move her food around, so she always knew where it was. But, it was the family time, the meals together that she cherished. If only all families ate together like we did.

Many people told me, "She'd starve if she were my bird." And, that's precisely why she wasn't. She was mine.

Chapter Twenty-Nine

The lure of the refrigerator

I could always tell Jaké was feeling better because just when one sort of drama was over, on came the hormones. And, when Jaké got hormonal, or laid claim to some area of the house, you'd better look out! She would protect it with every bit of strength her four little ounces could muster. I've been dive bombed from the cabinets, attacked head-on from counter level, and survived several sneak attacks from the rear. All in a day's work when you're protecting *Divatiel* territory.

Jaké had always been in love with dark places, and snooping them out was her specialty. It didn't mean that I approved of her choices, but sometimes she got around my desires.

For a few weeks, Jaké was intrigued by the dark space on the side of the refrigerator. I kept my step stool and dustpan there, but she didn't seem to be dissuaded. Every time I saw her snooping in that direction, I picked her up and talked to her.

"No, Jaké, it's dangerous to go there. You could get stuck and either be injured or I wouldn't be able to get you out. Stay away from the side of the refrigerator! Don't go there!!!"

But, we were dealing with an independent *Divatiel*, and when she made up her mind she wanted something, she got it. To her, getting to the back of that dark space by the refrigerator was like earning an Olympic gold medal. She had to have it, and she would do what it took to get it.

As long as I was home, I could keep her busy or at least try to block her path. But, when I was out, she didn't have the Momma to stand in her way.

One day I came home and I couldn't find her. I ran around the house calling for her, and she didn't answer. I was frantic! I looked every place I'd found her before, and several places I hadn't. No Jaké. I made another round around the house. Still no Jaké. I thought I was going to faint. Usually she yelled to me as soon as I came in the door, but I'd been home about 20 minutes already, and she was nowhere to be found. I was in the kitchen getting ready to dial my sister, when out from the side of the refrigerator sauntered my sneaky little birdie!

"You bad girl," I said. "You had Momma scared! Why didn't you answer Momma when I called? You know you're not supposed to go there!"

She looked at me, gave me her *'Chirp' of understanding*, and bowed her head for me to scratch. Then she flew to the table to get something to eat.

I was furious! It was bad enough she went to the one area I told her not to go. But the fact that she didn't answer me really made me mad.

So, I thought, *I'll take care of her. I'll block her path!*

Since Jaké was such a tiny little thing, I had to be careful not to put anything in a position that it might fall on her. And, if it did, that it wouldn't hurt her. Fat chance when it came to my smart little one.

The first thing I did was put the waste basket across the opening. It stood about two feet high and a foot wide, and hopefully, was too heavy for her to knock over.

I thought, *there you go you little sneak, try getting past that.*

It took her about an hour to figure out that she could use the basket as a launch pad. She would fly to the top of it, walk around the edge, and coast down on the other side. The problem was that there wasn't enough room for her to spread her wings and fly back out, and since the entrance was blocked by the basket, she couldn't walk out either. I didn't like that because I always wanted her to be able to get to her food and water.

So, Plan B. I took a paper grocery bag and, folded, stood it up across the opening. I then placed the dustpan up against the refrigerator to hold the bag in place. Jaké was intrigued and immediately thought she'd have this one conquered in no time, too. She flew to the top of the bag, but it didn't support her weight, and she fell down. Thinking it was a fluke, she gave it another shot with the same result.

Aha, I thought. *Gotcha!*

For several days, Jaké kept trying to get past the big, bad, brown paper bag, to no avail. Still, she was undeterred. She wanted to get back to her favorite new hiding place, and she'd figure out how to do it.

For a couple of weeks, I noticed that she was nibbling on the paper bag.

No big deal, I thought. *She nibbles on everything.*

Well, almost everything. I lucked out that she didn't have the habit of many cockatiels where she'd fly to the top of doors and slowly turn them into toothpicks. But paper – ah, she loved tearing apart paper. Still, I thought nothing of her nibbling on the grocery bag. I was certain that she'd realize she couldn't get past it and eventually turn her attention elsewhere.

Silly me! One day I was watching television when I heard a little "*flit.*" I'd never heard that sound before, so I was a bit concerned. I immediately started to call for Jaké. She wasn't answering.

Oh no, I thought, *another episode like the time she got caught in the cabinet.*

I got up and went into the kitchen. No Jaké. I kept calling for her. All of a sudden, I heard that little "*flit*" noise again. I looked down to see Jaké slink out from the side of the refrigerator. That little snot had nibbled a hole in the bag at just the right height so she could walk back and forth through it, using it like a swinging door, to get to that tempting dark corner. I couldn't believe it! She was so proud of herself, walking back and forth, paper bag swinging with electronic precision. She had her gold medal.

But, it appeared, one gold medal was not enough for my Olympic *Divatiel.* I flipped the bag around so it was solid against the opening again, but since she already had the formula down pat, it took her just a couple of days to rip a new hole in the bag. Back came the swinging door. But, this time, with a caveat.

Usually, as soon as I came home, I'd go into my bedroom, change into something comfortable, and put on my flip flops. This day was no different. Jaké had already called to me, so I knew she was okay, and I simply went into my room to change before heading into the kitchen. Big mistake.

Jaké decided that she was upset with me for the whole bag incident, so she must have spent the entire day plotting her revenge. When I walked into the kitchen, instead of receiving a lovey-dovey greeting, I was in immediate pain. Jaké had dug her beak into my big toe!

Ouch!

She looked up at me as if to say, "There. How do you like it?" and went back to her swinging door. As soon as I went near the refrigerator to get something to eat, she came rushing out from her hiding place, and swiftly placed her beak into the soft skin on top of my foot, the same place they always tell you is extremely painful to get a tattoo.

Ouch!

My precious little *Divatiel* had turned into a warrior! She was so mad at me; she not only wanted to protect her newly won territory, Jaké also wanted to lay claim to the entire kitchen! Let me tell you, it's a great diet plan. Jaké wouldn't let me get anywhere near the refrigerator.

I live in the desert. I wear flip flops. That means there's lots of exposed foot flesh. Bird beaks are small but powerful.

Ouch!

And, my feet were not enough for Jaké to conquer. She started biting and fighting with the dustpan. *Attack of the evil dustpan! Kill that dustpan!* It might just sneak up on her and claim her territory when she wasn't looking. And, when she was done fighting the dustpan, she immediately snuck around the corner of the kitchen island, found my feet and bit my toes. I didn't even have to move to be attacked. I'd just stand at my previously critical spot at the island doing my crossword puzzles, and there was Jaké, attacking my feet, just to make a point.

Stay out of my territory!

I finally started wearing tennis shoes when I got home, as this phase seemed to be lasting several days. She couldn't bite into the leather, so I was temporarily safe. However, I had to be careful not to step on her with my heavy shoes. I got into the habit of sliding my feet when I knew she was on the floor so I wouldn't accidentally injure her.

I resigned myself to the fact that Jaké was enjoying her little foray and it didn't appear to harm her in any way, so I just let her be. However, some nights she actually wanted to sleep there! That's where I drew the line. She needed to sleep in Momma's room on the shower door.

Jaké would go scurrying to her dark corner, and it was impossible for me to reach her. I'd take out the dreaded yard stick and poke it back there. It was a real skill to be able to drop the yard stick and pick her up at the same time, without allowing her to fly off. Some nights it would take two or three attempts. I didn't like to do anything to scare her or make her too mad, so I really hated using the yard stick, but I knew it was in her best interest to be out of the hole for the night.

Ouch!

It took Jaké approximately three seconds to sink her beak into my thumb. I walked quickly and let her fly up onto the shower door. Once there, she immediately turned around and flew to my shoulder whereupon she sunk her beak into my neck. Then she flew up onto the shower door, bowed down and spread her wings to tell me she loved me, walked to her corner and went to sleep.

Chapter Thirty

Redecorating

After we lived in the house for a few years, I decided to do a thorough cleaning and redecorating. That required painting as well as moving everything from every room in the house. For the most part, Jaké understood that things were a bit messy - not because we were moving, but because I was cleaning. However, there was one time that put her in such a state, I wasn't sure she'd ever be the same again.

The house originally had very light cream walls throughout, and my goal was to add a bit of color. I had just finished the hall bathroom, when I became energized to work on the master bedroom suite. I rounded up all the art and accessories in the room, and moved them into other parts of the house.

When it was time for Jaké to go nite-nite, she seemed a bit disoriented and her plume went up immediately. I explained to her that I was getting ready to start painting the room, so I had to remove everything from the walls. I didn't think it would be a big issue as she usually got scared when I added or moved things, not removed them.

However, this time was different. By the time I went to wake her in the morning, she looked as if she had suffered a stroke. She barely moved, and didn't want to eat or drink. Of course, it was a Sunday, and no avian vets worked on Sundays in this town. I started crying, and we sat in the living room watching television all day.

When Monday morning came, I quickly took her to my vet. She had no idea what had happened exactly, but when I explained to her the circumstances, she hazarded a guess.

"Cockatiels need to have contrast and textures in order to see," she said. "By removing everything and leaving the walls nearly white, as well as the tile and the sinks, it was as if she was suffering from snow blindness.

"She obviously is extremely disoriented and confused," she continued. "Whatever you do, don't do that again!"

I heeded the vet's advice, and put everything back into my bedroom as soon as I returned home. I thought Jaké would recover immediately, seeing that things were back to normal, but once again, I was tested.

It took Jaké nearly two weeks before she started to feel like herself again. She lost a lot of weight, almost dropping down to the weight of a normal cockatiel. It was really touch and go on some nights. I had no idea that such a minor thing as cleaning out a room would cause my baby such distress.

I delayed any decorating changes for a few weeks, until I knew that she was feeling better, and I decided to work on a different part of the house. My baby's health was definitely more important than painting that room at that exact time.

It also amazed me that I had known her for so long, yet I was still learning things about her and cockatiels in general. I assumed that since they fly so fast, they would have amazing eyesight. I never thought about the need to have that contrast and dimension.

I didn't know if that experience was exaggerated by her inability to see things at dusk. From the time I delighted in bringing her into my life, Jaké suffered from what appeared to be a vitamin A deficiency. As a result, as soon as it started to get dark, I had to make sure the lights were on. She just couldn't see otherwise. She'd stay put where she was until I put a little light on the area. Maybe it was because it's hard to see contrast at dusk, I just don't know.

I noticed, too, that when she flew, she wouldn't fly into a dark room. If she was mad at me and she took off for the comfort of the bathroom, she did a quick 180 if I hadn't yet turned on the lights in that room and it was after sundown.

She also had to have a night light when she was sleeping. In the beginning, I didn't think she needed it because she wasn't covered when she went nite-nite, but once I figured out all her needs, I discovered a night light was a requirement. I guess, out in the wild, there are stars, the moon and street lights, so it's never really totally dark.

In her advanced age, I realized that it was a bit more than just having a light on for comfort. She wanted to see. And, surprisingly, since she moved around a lot at night, I'm sure it kept her safe!

Jaké was more observant and occasionally listened better than some humans I know.

While in the midst of redecorating the house, I moved my home office from the front bedroom to the side one. The front bedroom was great for her because it was a straight shot to fly from the kitchen or living room. I'd had it there for over five years. So, when I decided to move my office, I was worried about how she would handle it.

In the old office, Jaké had a bookshelf all to herself, and lots of papers to rip up. She slept on the shelf, preened, and just watched me to make sure I wasn't leaving her. She sometimes flew to the floor and slept on the rung of my office chair. From a *Divatiel's* perspective, she was very content. Remember, birds don't like change.

However, I felt it was in my best interest to move my office to the side bedroom, so I started planning how to tell her. And, I made sure there was a shelf set aside for her in my new office, too.

Every few days, once the whole decorating process began, I walked Jaké to the new room while she was on my shoulder and told her this was now my office.

"When Mommy says she's in her office, this is the room you go to."

I walked her all around the room so she could see the layout of the furniture, and I also walked her from the kitchen and living room directly to my new office to show her how to get there. I hardly used the room before, so she wasn't used to the space.

Then, I walked her to my old office and told her that, "This isn't going to be Mommy's office any more. I'm going to use it as something else, so when Mommy says that she's in her office, don't come to this room anymore."

After a few weeks, I was finally ready to officially move my office. From the very first time I said that I was in my office when she called, Jaké made her way directly to my new office. Not once did she go to the original room.

Now, the angle was a bit difficult for her to cut at the speeds she flew, and being the smart cookie that she was, she figured it out before I did. So, she flew to the hallway as far as she could, landed on the floor and walked the rest of the way.

I was such a proud Mommy the first time I called to her and I saw her little grey head bopping its way into my office. She paid attention, followed directions, and found Mommy correctly the first time and every time.

Chapter Thirty-One

What a little smartie!

Who needs Punxsutawney Phil or Mojave Max when you have an intelligent *Divatiel* like Jaké to predict the weather? No, she didn't wake me up with a daily forecast. However, she did predict the change in seasons by the way she slept.

I noticed a few months into her habit of sleeping on the shower door that she periodically changed where she fell asleep. For example, if she was cuddled up against the interior wall of the shower for months on end, all of a sudden, with no prompting and for seemingly no reason, she would change positions and begin sleeping against the exterior shower wall. She'd be there for awhile, when once again, she'd move back to sleeping near the interior wall.

At first, I chalked this up to the idiosyncrasies of my little *Divatiel.* After all, she was going to sleep wherever she wanted when she wanted. I thought, perhaps, a light was shining in her eye, or it was quieter and she didn't hear the television if she slept against one wall or the other. I really had no idea why she was doing it.

I finally started to pay attention to the calendar and when I did, I realized that she was changing sleep positions at the turn of a new season. So, when it was time for the summer to heat up, she slept near the exterior wall. But when fall was on its way, she moved inward and slept against the interior wall of the house where it was definitely warmer.

Once I figured it out, I appreciated the heads up, far ahead of what the meteorologists could predict. Just like Jaké let me know about earthquakes, she also told me whether I should have the air conditioner or the furnace on!

I'm not sure how cockatiel habits differ in the wild when it comes to a change of season, but even in the wilds of Las Vegas, Jaké knew the best place to sleep.

Jaké and I had been together since 1993, and some things about our communication amazed me.

I was amazed at how vulnerable and trusting something so little could be compared to how big I was. I gave her lots of kisses, from the time she got up till the time she went nite-nite, and she accepted them with love. I could have easily opened my mouth just a little bit more, and swallowed her in a couple of bites, but she didn't even seem to ponder that, nor did I. She just sat on my hand and let me kiss her up a storm. I guess it's not unusual for bonding to occur between two such different species. You've all heard about Christian the lion, and the elephant and the dog, Tara and Bella. This was simply the *Divatiel and the Blonde*.

I've already told you about sleeping on the big bed together after she was injured. Now, that was a super big level of trust!

Yet, there was that lack of trust that came through, too. I could attempt to pick her up but if I didn't tell her where I was taking her, she was already plotting her escape route. If I was planning to give her a bit of calcium, I didn't even have to say anything. She sensed what I had in mind and off she went into hiding.

If I walked more than a few feet away from her, she either called to me or gave her little scared whimper, as if I would ever have left without telling her. Even when I said I was just going to the garage, she didn't believe me and oftentimes, when I got back in the house, she was already hiding. Then she'd come out and look at me like, "I knew that. I knew you were only going into the garage, just like you said you were."

If I put my finger down to scratch her head, she watched my hand very closely to make sure I wasn't going to grab her. Yes, I had done so in the past, but only because I needed to put her in her cage or to give her vitamins. It was amazing how one little incident could stay with her for life.

Since she'd never been covered in the cage, she had an aversion to towels or blankets. When I took her to the vet in the winter, I covered her cage with a blanket until we got into the car to keep her warm. She hated it! She yelled or pecked at the blanket until I uncovered her cage.

It's incredible that she knew how much I loved her and I'd taken care of her through so much, yet she didn't always trust me. I just don't understand. Maybe it was the *Divatiel* in her!

I had the pleasure of babysitting my niece's Jack Russell terrier for nearly two weeks. Surprisingly, he didn't react to the birds outside at all, but Jaké, well…he was fascinated with her. My vet said he probably thought she was a toy, so she intrigued him.

Jaké tried to be well-behaved and not tempt him too much. For the most part, she either stayed on top of the refrigerator or on top of the cabinets behind the silk plant in the corner, or in her basket. However, she really liked to eat a long dinner, so around 7 p.m., she'd fly down to her cage to eat. That would just set off the dog to no end.

I had two choices. I could hold him extremely tightly until she finished eating and was ready to go nite-nite, or I could put him in the kennel. Either way, he wasn't happy.

If I held him, he kept trying to get free, hoping I'd lose my grip. She'd already hit the floor a couple of times during his visit due to the lack of full throttle from her wings from molting. I, luckily, so far, had kept him from her, but when I'd hold him, his eyes were fixated on her the entire time, and he squirmed non-stop.

The nights I put him in the kennel, he barked incessantly for the entire time, sometimes two hours. And he was a dog who quietly and willingly stayed in his kennel for hours at home. Jaké seemed to understand that she was safe, and she also quite enjoyed the fact that he was stuck in the kennel.

I'd never seen her eat so slowly in my entire life! She'd take a bite, think a bit if she wanted more, preened a little, took a drink of water, took another bite, climbed on top of her cage to nibble on her lettuce, then back down for another bite or two, all the while his barking ringing throughout the house. Now, this was a bird who got frightened when the wind blew. Yet, she totally ignored his barking and just went about her business. It was as if she knew it was driving him crazy to be locked in the kennel on her behalf, and she quite enjoyed it.

Once she finished eating and preening and whatever, I'd put her nite-nite in the bedroom and shut the door so he couldn't get in. Then, I let him out of the kennel. He immediately ran to her table, ran around it, jumped on his hind legs to see if she was there as if to say, "Hey *Divatiel*! Because of you I'm locked in the kennel. I think we need to have a few words." But, thankfully, she was already nite-nite, and he eventually forgot about her until we went to sleep on the big bed.

We did the same routine every single night. You'd think he would realize that after a few days, and not bark, knowing he'd be let out as soon as she went nite-nite. But, nooooooo. Every single night, same story, same place, same barking, same defiance. That was my little *Divatiel*.

Chapter Thirty-Two

A princess till the end

It was a long while before the *Divatiel* and I were apart for any period of time again. Two years in fact. I made a trip home to visit my Mom in June of 2010, so Jaké went to spend the week with my sister.

Now, my sister knew not to burn any candles with Jaké around, so I was surprised that first morning after my return when I bent down to kiss Jaké, she smelled like soot or burned ash. I double checked with my sister and she said she followed my rules and didn't burn anything while I was out of town, especially candles. I was perplexed, but I thought, the ashy smell would go away. I missed her sweet smell.

I continued redecorating and painting the house. We were nearly finished! Painting the kitchen and dining area was difficult because it meant disrupting the princess's routine. And, we know how Jaké loved routine!

For one week, I had to keep her off the top of the cabinets. Everything was cleaned off, but I didn't want her walking up there with the dust from sanding and painting. I explained to Jaké that everything would look stunning, a palace fit for a princess, when all was complete. Still, she either clung to me, stayed near her cage or slept in the bathroom.

Once the kitchen was back together, I opted to paper the top of the cabinets before I put everything back. When I gave Jaké the OK to fly back up there, she was annoyed that it felt different than it did before. From my perspective, it would be easier to clean but I think she secretly liked the dust. It took her two weeks before she finally went back to her old routine.

We eventually had to go into the master bedroom and bath to paint. Luckily, we were able to keep my bed in there and just move it around while we worked, but I recalled the time when I cleared out all the decorations and I didn't want to put Jaké through that again. That meant a lot of work for me, but it was all worth it.

Every day before the painter came, I emptied the room. He did his work, gathered up the tarps, put away his painting supplies, and my work began. I was so worried about Jaké injesting any of the dust or paint that I completely mopped the entire house every single day while this room was being painted. Every day. Mopped. The entire floor.

And, once the floor was mopped, I returned all the art and decorations back to their original locations in the room. That way, when Jaké went to sleep, it was as normal as possible from her perspective. I also used an extremely environmentally-friendly paint so there were no vapors to bother my little baby.

It took until September to finish that side of the house. I was exhausted! And, we were heading into the time of year when Jaké often had episodes of not feeling well. Fall, for some reason, always seemed to be a tough time. Sure enough, on a Friday night, I noticed that her droppings were really liquid.

It wasn't the first time it happened, but I hated when these things occurred to her on a weekend because I couldn't get any medical help for her. Droppings can help indicate the health of a bird, so it's really important to watch what they look like. Watery droppings were not a good thing, but if it was just for an hour or two, she should be okay.

I hoped that by morning her droppings would improve. Every now and then one looked normal, but for the most part, they seemed rather liquidy. I also noticed she was drinking a bit more than usual.

When Monday came, I quickly took her to the vet. I'd been going there for a long time now, so she knew Jaké and me very well. Her words were much like what she had told me the last time we faced such a dire situation. Jaké is old. We can do tests, but there's a good chance they might be inconclusive. The tests themselves could prove to be harmful to Jaké and could put her in a worse state. I'd heard it all before. Those weren't the words I wanted to hear. I wanted to know that she would be okay.

I took Jaké home with orders from my vet to keep an eye on her. We were to return in a few days so she could check her weight. If she was losing weight, that was a bad sign.

We did as we were told. Jaké's droppings were intermittently better, but for the most part they were still watery. I knew what that meant. I just didn't want to accept it.

We weighed her and her weight remained constant. It was up to me. I could maintain the quality of life Jaké currently had, perhaps with the chance that she'd improve, or I could put her through some miserable tests and maybe lose her in the process. I opted to keep things the way they were and to love her as much as I possibly could every single day. I wanted her to get better. I tried to will her better. But, in my heart, I just knew.

I had a feeling that something was wrong, that it was her time to go and leave me to fend for myself. She was showing signs of kidney issues, and at her age, that was not a good thing. It also meant that her time on this earth was not long.

Over the next couple of months, so many things changed. She spent more time walking around and looking for dark corners than she did flying. When I'd go out, I had to lock her in her cage. Otherwise, she would fly to the floor as soon as I left the house, then she couldn't reach her food and water on top of the table. I knew she hated being locked up, but it was the only way I knew she could eat and drink. I wasn't out that long, but I just wanted to make sure she had access to everything she needed. It also gave her a chance to sit near her grow light, a habit she, too, had avoided for several weeks.

She wasn't as independent. She clung to me like she never did before. She hadn't gone on top of the kitchen cabinets for weeks. She wasn't preening as often. Her chirp was a bit weaker. And her sweet smell had all but disappeared. I would know. I kissed her every chance I got.

She looked the same. She hissed the same. She still had a youthful spirit. But, when she ate, she would only do so propped on my shoulder. I'd sit in our favorite chair in front of the television and position her and her food dish on my left shoulder. She'd eat for a bit, then pause. That was my cue to put the water dish in front of her for a drink. Then she'd eat for a bit more. She didn't even eat her treats for a couple of weeks. That was highly unusual. Not a day went by she didn't have lettuce breath.

She also wanted to eat and drink more often. I think that was partly her way of making sure that I still cared because it was something we had to do together. Besides her three or four meals, she'd yell in the middle of the night. She wanted a drink. Of course, I immediately got her water dish and brought it to her.

When I worked at my computer, she didn't sit on my knee or my shoulder any more. Instead, she sat at my feet on the floor. She wanted to be near me, but perhaps, my movements were too much for her to handle in her condition.

She flew around a little bit. In fact, she finally learned to cut that sharp corner to fly directly into my office. For the most part, she walked. She'd yell, to tell me it was time for lunch or dinner, or she was thirsty, and she'd walk in the direction of the living room. She'd stop to make sure I was following her, then kept yelling and walking. Then she'd just stop and give me that "Mommy up!" look for me to pick her up.We did this nearly every day for the few weeks before she left.

When it became obvious she wouldn't be around much longer, I had a talk with her a few days before her passing. I told her I didn't want her to suffer, and if she had to leave me, I understood. I thanked her for her love and told her it would be okay.

For a couple of days, I don't think she slept at all. She usually took several naps, but all of a sudden, she didn't take any. It was as if she wanted to capture every last possible moment here on earth.

The two nights before she passed away, she didn't even hiss at me when she was sleeping. She just stayed curled up on the shower door. She'd look at me with that *Eagle Eye*, but she didn't hiss. That just wasn't normal.

The night before she died, I had a dream that she was throwing up. She had never thrown up her entire life. She had that one incident with food stuck in her crop, but that was it. She didn't die in my dream, but that's exactly how she would.

It was about 9:30 p.m. Wednesday night. I was getting her ready to go nite-nite, wiping down the shower area from her droppings from the previous night. I tried to keep the shower clean so I could track the changes in her droppings and know what to tell the vet.

She slid off my shoulder onto the floor screaming and flapping. She threw up three times. Her poor body was contorted, and she looked at me with pleading eyes.

"Mommy, help! Mommy, pick me up and make it all better!"

In a few moments, she would die in my arms. She was already pretty lifeless when I picked her up and held her to my chest. She looked at me with one eye, perhaps a final plea, or maybe just a final look. Then she closed her eyes and tucked her head under her wing. After one final breath, my precious angel was gone.

I screamed so loud and so deeply, I was afraid my neighbors would be frightened. I cried and shook and cried again. It couldn't be true. Jaké and I were together for so long, I just couldn't imagine not having her with me.

When I could finally pry her away and placed her on the counter, I could see that she was still very regal even in her last moments. Her head was curled down under an extended wing, her plume feathers high, her feet pointed and crossed, almost like a ballerina.

I'm grateful I was there for her, both in life and in death. I'm glad that I could hold her for her final breath. I'm glad that I was the last thing that she saw before she closed her eyes. I just wish she didn't have to go.

I spoke with her vet who thought perhaps she had a heart attack. No one will ever know. The only thing I do know is that I miss her terribly. It's quiet and lonely here without her. It's amazing how much impact four ounces of feathers and determination can have on your life.

I hardly slept that first night, and cried my eyes raw. I finally stopped shaking and hyperventilating. I took her to the cemetery to be cremated. I wrote a note to her from Mommy to be included in the cremation, along with a few strands of my hair and some branches from her favorite basket. It broke my heart to leave her. I wanted her here with me.

I hated the fact I couldn't pick her up from the cemetery the next day. They had too many cremations in line before Jaké and I had to wait. They were closed on the weekend, so it would be

Monday before I could bring her home. I felt her calling me, like she was lonely, or looking for her mate. I counted the hours until she could be home again.

The cemetery does a very nice keepsake for pet owners. They take foot prints and add a lock of the hair or in Jaké's case, feathers. I told them not to touch a feather on her precious little head. She came into this world in one piece, and she would go out a princess, with every feather on her body intact. Besides, I have an entire shoe box full of her feathers. I don't know why I'd need them to take another from her.

Jaké was very lucky. She was old. Very old. Twenty-one and a half years old. That's about 105 in human years. She had a good quality of life all the way until the end. She did have cataracts in both eyes, which might explain her preference to walk rather than fly in her later days, although her vision seemed to be fine and she always got where she wanted to go.

She wasn't hospitalized or medicated. All her feathers were perfect. Some older birds look scraggly or even naked because they can't produce new feathers after a molt in their old age, but not my *Divatiel*. She didn't suffer from arthritis or any other issues so many older cockatiels deal with. But none of that matters. Jaké is gone.

Every day for as long as I had Jaké, the grow light on her table burned for hours. That first day, I didn't turn it on. It felt extremely lonely and cold. The second day I decided to turn it on and I felt a bit calmer. Sure, I was doing things like looking for her to put her nite-nite and I could hear her calling me.

"Mommy, where are you? I need you!"

I can still hear her little feet on the shower as she walked from side to side, or the rustle of her feathers from preening. I don't remember the hisses, but I do remember the kisses. The softness of her feathers. Her sweet smell. The way she rubbed her head against my neck and preened my hair.

I know grieving is a process. I actually slept the second night and laughed a little bit when I thought about all the wonderful experiences we shared. The one that comes to mind for some reason is when I had company and she would hang on my shirt in the middle of my back to hide. She knew I couldn't reach her back there, and she used my body as protection against the stranger. Then, when she got brave, she'd climb up just a bit and sneak a peek over my shoulder. If she didn't like what she saw, back to the middle she went.

My sister recalled the time she came out to California to help me get my new house together. We were hanging some artwork, and one of the paintings was placed above my dresser, just above where Jaké's cage went for nite-nite. She hated change, particularly something that invaded her personal space. When I put Jake nite-nite, her eyes widened, her plume went up, and her whole body became erect. I think she stayed that way all night, poor thing, but she eventually got used to it being there. I know now that a detailed explanation would have helped.

A friend of mine reminded me about her memorable encounter with Jaké. She didn't know Jaké was flighted. She thought I clipped her wings. She came over for a visit and who came flying down the hallway but my little *Divatiel*! My friend was caught off guard and scared of this flying creature. She thought it was a bat! She started waving her arms in self-defense. Jaké got scared and fell to the floor. I scooped up Jaké and yelled at my friend for scaring her, while she yelled at me for Jaké scaring *her*! We laughed. Every situation has its perspective.

It's just amazing how kind some people can be when I tell them about her passing, and how inconsiderate others are. That's okay. They don't deserve the love of someone like Jaké.

Whenever I was sad, Jaké was always there to comfort me. She just knew that I needed a little extra lovin' at times. She'd fly to my shoulder and rub her head against my neck, or she'd lay across my chest and give me a hug. Who's there to comfort me now? When my father passed away, I could swear that she cried along with me. I never before heard the sounds she made at that time, nor did I ever again. I didn't realize a bird could feel such emotion. We were bonded, definitely.

I went to *Things Remembered* and purchased a very *Divatiel*-esque keepsake box for her ashes, inscribed:

Jaké

My precious little Divatiel

1989 – 2010

It's silver with a pearlized finish set with Swarovski crystals and a teardrop shaped pearl. It's heart shaped, as is the inscription plate. It makes me smile every time I look at it. She deserved only the most beautiful, and no pet urn could compare.

I was an absolute wreck until I brought her home. I cried so much in the car once I picked her up at the cemetery, I was afraid to drive. Then a funny thing happened. Once she was home, I became calm. Content. My baby was with me once again.

I called Tim Link to see if he could chat with her. I just wanted to make sure Jaké was okay. I needed to know she wasn't hurt in any way, and that all was well with her. Tim spoke with her and said she's fine, that she had an interesting life with me, and that she was with me. I believe.

I had a dream about her. She was flying around in all her glory. Yay for Jaké!

I know in no uncertain terms that my life is better today because for 17 years I had one of the most precious gifts anyone can have – unconditional love. To think that such a tiny, feathered creature could bring such joy to my life. I only pray that she is in a good place, in good health, watching over me with all the other angels.

Jaké Maciolek

May 1, 1989 – November 3, 2010

Lessons from the Divatiel

Be gentle.

Everyday we're told to push harder, faster, stronger. But, taking care of a creature as fragile as a cockatiel requires you to connect with your gentler side. Their egos and energy make them appear that they're stronger than they really are. Rather than grabbing my baby, I loved to have her simply climb onto my hand, up my arm, across my shoulders. If you are gentle with them, they will teach you so much more. Be gentle with others and you will find yourself less stressed and happier.

Be persistent.

I can't help but recall the whole paper bag incident. Jaké was so determined to find her way into the dark corner beside the refrigerator, she never thought of walking away from that paper bag. Every day she took just one or two little bites out of it, and soon enough, a hole big enough for her to crawl through emerged. When I flipped the bag, she already knew how to get past my ploy. How many of us give up because it seems as if we'll never reach our goal? Just think of Jaké with her paper bag and keep moving forward.

Be patient.

I had the opportunity to tease my brain with crossword puzzles waiting patiently for Jaké to finish eating. Day after day after day. She just didn't want me to move. She wanted me to wait there for her. So, instead of stewing, I found something useful to do with my time. Patience can be learned. Don't constantly complain when you have to wait. Find a way to make that gift of time valuable to you.

Be accepting.

We've been in the 'me' decade for several decades now. Everything is about us. We put ourselves before everyone else and if we don't like what's happening, instead of pushing through it, we move on. Birds like Jaké are very demanding and bonding, and let you know that at times, it's all about them. By accepting that they need love and attention, and letting them run the show a little bit, it's rewarding to put someone else's needs first.

Be loving.

How many hugs or kisses have you given today? How many times have you told someone, "I love you?" Have you felt that love returned? I guarantee not a day went by when Jaké did not receive at least 25 kisses and I told her "Momma loves you" as many times. She reciprocated by showing she loved me in her own way – rubbing her head on my neck, giving me an angel hug, bowing and showing her feathers, calling for me. Even lecturing was her way of showing me love. Give love and you'll get it back – and more – in return.

Be real.

Birds are very astute. And, yes, people are, too. We can feel other's energy, good or bad, happy or sad. Jaké was always very good about reading my energy. I had to really focus to change my energy and keep it clean around her as much as possible. I didn't want her to worry or be stressed about something she couldn't do anything about. Others can read your energy as well, so be real and be positive.

Be aware.

Jaké was always aware of the littlest change in movement or surroundings. Although she wasn't like many dogs I've known who bark at falling leaves, she did notice things and let me know. Whether it was the neighbor walking in the backyard, the phone ringing, the doorbell, or even the egret who ate my fish, Jaké let me know. She also had what I consider a photographic memory. Anything that was in a different place than before was noticed nearly instantly by her. I suspect it's a skill birds have because they fly and they need to know safe paths. Always be aware of what is normal and what is different about your surroundings.

Be inquisitive.

Many people are content to just get up, go to work or school, come home, watch television or play video games, go back to bed and start over again tomorrow. Being inquisitive keeps you young, alive and interesting to others. Learning does not end when you graduate from school. It's lifelong. Jaké was always snooping, trying new things – although I could never get her to eat fruit – flying new routes, changing up her routine. I'm sure her sense of adventure and curiosity is part of what kept her going all those years.

Be considerate.

Do you refuse to call people to let them know you're running late? Do you take the last cup of coffee and not refill the pot for someone else? Do you control the remote? Do you refuse to turn the heat up? I could go on and on. There are so many ways people are inconsiderate to others. I always let Jaké know when I was going out, how long I'd be gone, if I knew a visitor was coming over, what time we had to get up in the morning and so on. And, I was always ready to offer an apology when I did something she didn't like. Consideration is part of respect and trust and that helps to build strong relationships.

Be balanced.

Jaké had quite an active day, but she also made sure she got plenty of rest. I'm not sure birds in the wild take naps during the day, but to Jaké, if that meant she could spend time with me, she napped! Many people are burning the candle at both ends, multitasking, going, going, going. It really is important to strike a balance. Work hard, play hard, sleep. You'll be glad you did.

Be assertive.

No one ever got anywhere by being quiet. Jaké was always good about letting me know what she wanted, in no uncertain terms. Whether that meant to give her treats or turn down the volume on the radio, she let me know. It wasn't always a loud chirp. Sometimes, it was a calm almost conversational tone. Know what you want. Go for it. And, let others know so they can help you achieve your goals.

Be wary.

It's good to know what's right and what's wrong, whom to trust and when to go the other direction. My little baby hid in the middle of my back when someone she considered a stranger came to visit. She trusted me, but that didn't mean she felt comfortable with everyone who walked in the door. Heck, she even hissed at the wonderful carpenter who rescued her from the kitchen cabinet. I often feared she'd step off the back of the refrigerator into the dark abyss she was drawn to so much. Luckily, she was wary. Something told her not to do it, and for that, I'm thankful.

Be you.

Each and every one of us is individual, unique, special. It's up to us to share our specialness with the world. That's what makes the world such a beautiful place. There will never be another Jaké, and for that, I'm grateful. She shared her wonderful personality with me and everyone who crossed her path. And, she often reminded me just how special she was. Release your inner Jaké and share yourself with the world. Maybe someone will write a book about you someday!

Things I miss

- Her overall presence
- That "Come and get me" chirp in the morning
- My nap buddy
- The "Welcome Home" chirp when I walk in the door
- Scratching her head
- Hearing the rustling of her feathers after preening
- Seeing her on the shower door at night
- Her preening on top of her cage
- Peeking from the plant in the corner of the cabinets
- Peeking from the hole in her basket on top of the cabinets
- Her "yelling" at me to do her bidding
- Taking care of her
- Buying fresh treats every couple of days
- Rushing home to be with her
- Watching her sometimes fall asleep while eating
- Finding out what new new thing she'd discover
- Giving her kisses
- The softness of her feathers
- Her sweet smell
- Her ability to trust someone several times her size
- A reason to turn on her grow light
- The sound of her little feet pacing across the top of the cabinets
- Jake'

Acknowledgements

Anyone who knows me knows this whole process has been a labor of love. This book has been in the making for 18 years, ever since Jaké came into my life. The more I wrote, the more I remembered. There are, I'm certain, stories I forgot to include, but I'm sure you now have a better understanding of my life with the *Divatiel* after reading this book.

I want to thank all my family, friends, co-workers and strangers alike who allowed me to regale them with stories of her antics and accomplishments. They told me I should write a book, and I finally did.

Thanks particularly to my family for allowing me not only to operate in "Jaké time," but to put up with my supposed eccentricities in regard to her.

Thanks to William who gave up this beautiful creature and gifted her to me. What a synchronistic event!

Thank you to my first vet who taught me the very stringent rules to take care of my new roommate. I learned because I loved my baby, and I'm forever grateful.

Thank you to the vet who performed her egg-bound surgery. Jaké could have been a goner many years earlier, but thanks to you, she made it through with flying colors, pun intended.

Thank you to the vet who took great care of her during the several years before her passing. Your skills as well as your kindness and compassion will always be remembered.

Thanks to the many people who reviewed the book, including family members Elaine and Marléna, to determine if I forgot any interesting stories; my vet to make sure everything I said was avian correct; Tim Link who did wonders for my baby and has much experience from writing his own books; and to William who gifted me with Jaké and wanted to learn about her wonderful and interesting life.

Thanks to my nephew, Daniel, for gifting me with the book's subtitle. It's perfect!

Thanks to Shelly Volsche for creating the logo of my precious Jaké that defines *Divatiel.* She also designed the book cover and did the layout. You're awesome! I couldn't have done this without you.

Thanks to Valory Degree, my editor. Without you, I'm not sure I would have ever finished. Thanks for all your help and guidance!

Thanks to Jackie Carpenter who took the photo of Jaké and me on the back cover. I love that photo! It's been sitting in a frame on my desk all these years. You're the only one who ever took photos of my baby and me, so I really cherish them.

If you were one of those unsuspecting seatmates on many an airplane, my thanks for allowing me to be a proud Momma and share my love for my baby with you.

Thanks to all who buy and read this book and share Jaké with others. She and I both appreciate it.

And, of course, I want to thank my loving roommate of 17 years, without whom my life would have taken a different path, but I'm grateful for the one I got to share with you.

About the Author

Cindi hails from Detroit, but now resides in Las Vegas, Nevada. After graduating from Michigan State University, Cindi first made her way to California where she utilized her creative talents in marketing and public relations for high tech companies. She also co-anchored a cable news show for over two years.

Cindi was a contributing art writer for *The Robb Report* for many years. She's had articles published by the *Old Farmer's Almanac*, *Delta Sky Magazine*, *Luxury Las Vegas Magazine* and syndicated by *The New York Times*.

Cindi's first CD, *Java Jems: 5 Minute Inspirations for Busy People*, is a unique combination of spoken word and original music. It was nominated for an album of the year award in 2006 by Just Plain Folks. Her first book, *The Basics of Buying Art*, is sold out. More books and screenplays are in development.

Her travels have taken her to 23 countries in North America, Europe and Asia.

Keep up-to-date with Cindi on her website at www.cindimaciolek.com.

Did you enjoy Divatiel?

Spread the word! Share your thoughts on Twitter, Facebook, LinkedIn or your blog.

Be sure to share your stories with us on **www.divatiel.com/stories**.

Also, if you have a photo of you holding *Divatiel* or photos of your precious animal friends, please submit them to *photos@divatiel.com.*

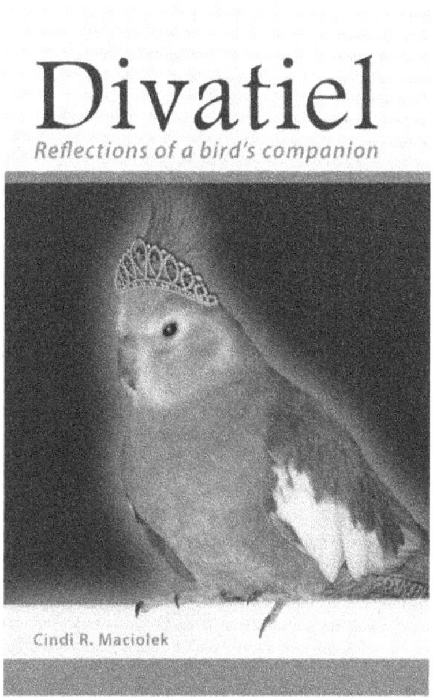

Divatiel is great for

- Book clubs
- Gift bags
- Fundraisers
- Corporate gifts

Contact Grand Arbor Press, LLC for discounts on volume purchases. Visit **www.grandarborpress.com** for contact information.

Be sure to check out **www.divatiel.com** for updates regarding the book and merchandise.

www.ingramcontent.com/pod-product-compliance
Lightning Source LLC
Chambersburg PA
CBHW051827090426
42736CB00011B/1683
* 9 7 8 0 9 6 4 7 9 1 1 3 8 *